THIS BOOK BELONGS TO

_____

START DATE

_____

SHE READS TRUTH

EXECUTIVE

FOUNDER/CHIEF EXECUTIVE OFFICER
Raechel Myers

CO-FOUNDER/CHIEF CONTENT OFFICER
Amanda Bible Williams

CHIEF OPERATING OFFICER
Ryan Myers

EXECUTIVE ASSISTANT
Sarah Andereck

EDITORIAL

EDITORIAL DIRECTOR
Jessica Lamb

MANAGING EDITOR
Beth Joseph

CONTENT EDITOR
Kara Gause

ASSOCIATE EDITORS
Bailey Gillespie
Tameshia Williams

EDITORIAL ASSISTANT
Hannah Little

CREATIVE

CREATIVE DIRECTOR
Jeremy Mitchell

LEAD DESIGNER
Kelsea Allen

DESIGNERS
Abbey Benson
Davis Camp DeLisi
Annie Glover

JUNIOR DESIGNER
Lauren Haag

MARKETING

MARKETING MANAGER
Katie Matuska Pierce

COMMUNITY SUPPORT SPECIALIST
Margot Williams

SHIPPING & LOGISTICS

LOGISTICS MANAGER
Lauren Gloyne

CUSTOMER SUPPORT SPECIALISTS
Elise Matson
Katy McKnight

FULFILLMENT LEAD
Abigail Achord

FULFILLMENT SPECIALISTS
Cait Baggerman
Noe Sanchez

SUBSCRIPTION INQUIRIES
orders@shereadstruth.com

CONTRIBUTORS

ARTWORK
Hayley Sheldon (6, 18, 46–47, 70, 78,
100, 114, 140, 148, 174, 180)

PHOTOGRAPHY
Rachel Novak Rust (65)
Vanessa Todd (41, 85, 127)

RECIPES
Abby Turner

@SHEREADSTRUTH

Download the
She Reads Truth app,
available for iOS
and Android

Subscribe to the
She Reads Truth podcast

SHEREADSTRUTH.COM

Research support provided by Logos Bible Software™. Learn more at logos.com.

Though the dates in this book have been carefully researched, scholars disagree on the dating of many New Testament events.

This book was printed offset in Nashville, Tennessee, on 70# Lynx Opaque. Cover is 100# Cougar Opaque with a soft touch lamination.

THIS IS THE NEW TESTAMENT

A BIBLICAL SURVEY OF THE NEW TESTAMENT

SHE READS TRUTH

The Bible isn't just a book of books.
It's our redemption story.

Amanda

Amanda Bible Williams
CO-FOUNDER & CHIEF
CONTENT OFFICER

Do you ever find yourself reading Scripture but not really understanding it? Looking, but not really seeing?

When I was a kid, there was a popular line of pictures called Magic Eye, art prints in which three-dimensional images were hidden among repeated and seemingly meaningless two-dimensional patterns. To see the hidden image, the viewer has to momentarily resist focusing on the details of the pattern and instead look through it, relaxing their focus and allowing the true image to emerge. They were notoriously difficult to see on your first try. But, once you got the hang of it, the entire Magic Eye world was your oyster.

Apart from giving us some terrible art for our walls, the thing that fascinates me most about this 1990s phenomenon is that it taught a whole generation a new way to see, literally training our eyes to see things we didn't know how to see before.

In some ways, this Study Book reminds me of the Magic Eye poster that hung on my bedroom wall back in high school (which was of a dolphin, by the way). It gives us a new way of seeing Scripture—a way that perhaps we didn't have before. It focuses our eyes on a holistic view of the Bible, a solid foundation on which to build a lifetime of reading and studying God's Word. Together with **This Is the Old Testament**, the first book in this two-part series, **This Is the New Testament** teaches the big picture of the Bible by surveying the purpose and theme of all sixty-six books and showing how they fit together to tell God's story of redemption.

I hope you're ready for an adventure over the next five weeks! In **This Is the New Testament**, we'll walk from Matthew all the way to Revelation, seeing Jesus's life, death, and resurrection unfold, watching as the Holy Spirit enables Jesus's disciples to spread His gospel, and reading the God-inspired letters and books that have instructed and encouraged the Church from the first century until now. Along the way, we'll grab hold of a key verse from each book so that, when we put them all together, we can see the full arc of Scripture.

The Bible isn't just a book of books. It's our redemption story. It's the story of how God has been working all things together for His glory and our good since before the foundation of the world. It's the story of how He is faithful to keep every promise He's ever made. And when we understand how it fits together, it forever changes not only the way we read Scripture, but also the way we see the world around us.

Sixty-six books. One story. Let's read it together.

At She Reads Truth, we believe in pairing the inherently beautiful Word of God with the aesthetic beauty it deserves. Each of our resources is thoughtfully and artfully designed to highlight the beauty, goodness, and truth of Scripture in a way that reflects the themes of each curated reading plan.

You'll find that many of the designs from **This Is the Old Testament** are also featured in this Study Book. This continuity reflects the way in which both the Old and New Testaments come together to form the complete narrative of the Bible. Our watercolor elements are inspired by artist Hayley Sheldon, whose own artwork is also highlighted throughout the book. The colors in her Shape Screen pieces inspired the five key colors we use to distinguish the five literary genres in this study (see page 16 for more about genres in the New Testament).

Hayley Sheldon

ARTIST

Hayley Sheldon is a multidisciplinary sculptor and installation artist focused on tactility and color. Her Shape Screens series, featured in this book, explores a vocabulary of repeated shapes with subtle palettes referencing the beauty of fleeting experiences in the natural world, like the slow growth of plant life or the gentle shift of sunset to dusk. Once distilled to discrete shapes and palettes, these individual building blocks are constructed into new visual experiences. She lives and works in West Palm Beach, Florida, with her husband and two daughters.

Abby Turner

RECIPES

Abby Turner is a somewhat-young professional who is loving life as a food blogger, Christian speaker, and author of her first cookbook, *The Living Table*. Her cookbook features over one hundred quick and easy recipes, along with devotionals, for everyday gatherings like pool parties and Tuesday game nights. She lives in Northwest Arkansas with her two papillons, Baylor and Mowgli, and enjoys a peppermint latte almost every morning.

HOW TO USE THIS BOOK

She Reads Truth is a community of women dedicated to reading the Word of God every day. The Bible is living and active, and we confidently hold it higher than anything we can do or say.

READ & REFLECT

Your **This Is the New Testament** Study Book focuses primarily on Scripture, with bonus resources to facilitate deeper engagement with God's Word. Each day you will read a key verse and thematic Scripture from each New Testament book. As you read, you'll discover a framework for your future study of each book of the Bible and gain a broader understanding of the story of the New Testament.

SCRIPTURE READING

Designed for a Monday start, this Study Book presents key passages from each book of the New Testament, along with supplemental passages that show how the theme of each day's reading can be found throughout Scripture.

DAILY REFLECTION

Each weekday features a unique question and a repeated question to guide you through the daily reading along with space to respond.

COMMUNITY & CONVERSATION

Join women from Beebe to the Bahamas as they read with you!

 SHE READS TRUTH APP

For added community and conversation, join us in the **This Is the New Testament** reading plan on the She Reads Truth app. You can also participate in community discussions, download free lock screens for Weekly Truth memorization, and more.

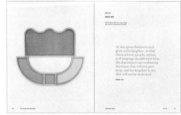

EXTRAS

Each day you will be directed to write the day's key verse in the space provided at the back of your book.

This book also features additional tools to help you gain a deeper understanding of your daily reading. See a complete list of extras in this book on page 10.

GRACE DAY

Use Saturdays to catch up on your reading, pray, and rest in the presence of the Lord.

WEEKLY TRUTH

Sundays are set aside for Scripture memorization. In this study, you'll memorize a portion of Paul's sermon in Acts 13, a short summary of the role Israel played in Christ's death, burial, and resurrection.

 SHEREADSTRUTH.COM

All of our reading plans are also available for free at SheReadsTruth.com. Invite your family, friends, and neighbors to read along with you!

 SHE READS TRUTH PODCAST

Join our She Reads Truth founders and their guests each Monday as they open their Bibles and talk about the beauty, goodness, and truth they find there. Each podcast episode corresponds to the current community reading plan. Subscribe on your favorite podcast app so you don't miss a conversation about **This Is the New Testament** and more.

Table of Contents

Triple Berry Salad
with Candied Pecans

PAGE 77

Mini Pizza Popovers

PAGE 113

Peach Crumble

PAGE 147

Let the word of Christ
dwell richly among you.

COLOSSIANS 3:16

A NOTE ABOUT New Testament Genres

The Bible is one complete work, made up of sixty-six smaller works, written over more than fifteen centuries. Because the Bible is made up of these individual books, the genres, or literary styles, vary throughout the texts of the Old and New Testaments. Knowing the type of literature we're reading helps us understand how to read it, keeping in mind the context, meaning, and intent of the original text. The guide on the following page offers a basic framework for approaching various literary styles.

In your daily reading, you'll notice the genre of each featured book is named on each day. The days are also color-coded to reflect which genre you are reading! Refer back to this guide as you need to over the next five weeks.

GOSPELS

The Gospels present the life and teachings of Jesus Christ and contain narratives, parables, and exhortations. Read the Gospels understanding they are the good news of the life, death, and resurrection of Jesus Christ.

CHURCH HISTORY

The book of Acts gives the history of the early Church, from Jesus's ascension to Paul's ministry in Rome. Read Acts to learn more about Peter and Paul and the work of the Holy Spirit to spread the message of the resurrected Christ.

PAULINE EPISTLES

The Pauline Epistles are letters written by the apostle Paul to leaders and members of the early Church. Read the Pauline Epistles understanding the historical, geographical, and spiritual context in which they were written, making sure to read each letter as a whole for the most complete understanding.

GENERAL EPISTLES

The General Epistles are letters written to early Christians in response to specific needs or circumstances. Read the General Epistles understanding the historical, geographical, and spiritual context in which they were written, making sure to read each letter as a whole for the most complete understanding.

APOCALYPTIC

The book of Revelation, a combination of prophecy and apocalyptic literature, is a letter written by the apostle John based on revelations from God. Read this complex book with humility, understanding that it, too, points to the good news and reveals Jesus Christ as King of kings, the Alpha and the Omega.

From then on Jesus began to preach, "Repent, because the kingdom of heaven has come near."

MATTHEW 4:17

Gospels

This tells you the genre for the featured book of the Bible you'll be reading each day. (See page 16 for more about New Testament genres.)

Matthew

WHAT IS MATTHEW?

The Gospel of Matthew is a testimony of Jesus's life and ministry told from the eyewitness perspective of Matthew, a Jewish tax collector who became a disciple of Jesus. This Gospel affirms Jesus as the Messiah promised in the Old Testament, and the reigning King who inaugurated the kingdom of God on earth. It also describes Jesus coming to call His people to turn away from their sin and toward Him.

This section gives you a short summary of each New Testament book.

MATTHEW 3:1-3

THE HERALD OF THE MESSIAH

¹ In those days John the Baptist came, preaching in the wilderness of Judea ² and saying, "Repent, because the kingdom of heaven has come near!" ³ For he is the one spoken of through the prophet Isaiah, who said:

A voice of one crying out in the wilderness:
Prepare the way for the Lord;
make his paths straight!

These primary passages offer context for the key verse.

MATTHEW 4:12-25

MINISTRY IN GALILEE

¹² When he heard that John had been arrested, he withdrew into Galilee. ¹³ He left Nazareth and went to live in Capernaum by the sea, in the region of Zebulun and Naphtali. ¹⁴ This was to fulfill what was spoken through the prophet Isaiah:

¹⁵ Land of Zebulun and land of Naphtali,
along the road by the sea, beyond the Jordan,
Galilee of the Gentiles.
¹⁶ The people who live in darkness
have seen a great light,
and for those living in the land of the shadow of death,
a light has dawned.

KEY VERSE

¹⁷ From then on Jesus began to preach, "Repent, because the kingdom of heaven has come near."

The key verse for each book of the Bible is marked in your reading. All together, the key verses from the Old and New Testaments tell the story of redemption from Genesis to Revelation.

THE FIRST DISCIPLES

¹⁸ As he was walking along the Sea of Galilee, he saw two brothers, Simon (who is called Peter), and his brother Andrew. They were casting a net into the sea—for they were fishermen. ¹⁹ "Follow me," he told them, "and I will make you fish for people." ²⁰ Immediately they left their nets and followed him.

²¹ Going on from there, he saw two other brothers, James the son of Zebedee, and his brother John. They were in a boat with Zebedee their father, preparing their nets, and he called them. ²² Immediately they left the boat and their father and followed him.

TEACHING, PREACHING, AND HEALING

²³ Now Jesus began to go all over Galilee, teaching in their synagogues, preaching the good news of the kingdom, and healing every disease and sickness among the people. ²⁴ Then the news about him spread throughout Syria. So they brought to him all those who were afflicted, those suffering from various diseases and intense pains, the demon-possessed, the epileptics, and the paralytics. And he healed them. ²⁵ Large crowds followed him from Galilee, the Decapolis, Jerusalem, Judea, and beyond the Jordan.

These supplemental passages from other places in the Bible show how the book's theme is present throughout Scripture.

EZEKIEL 18:21-32

²¹ "But if the wicked person turns from all the sins he has committed, keeps all my statutes, and does what is just and right, he will certainly live; he will not die. ²² None of the transgressions he has committed will be held against him. He will live because of the righteousness he has practiced. ²³ Do I take any pleasure in the death of the wicked?" This is the declaration of the Lord GOD. "Instead, don't I take pleasure when he turns from his ways and lives? ²⁴ But when a righteous person turns from his righteousness and acts unjustly, committing the same detestable acts that the wicked do, will he live? None of the righteous acts he did will be remembered. He will die because of the treachery he has engaged in and the sin he has committed.

25 "But you say, 'The Lord's way isn't fair.' Now listen, house of Israel: Is it my way that is unfair? Instead, isn't it your ways that are unfair? 26 When a righteous person turns from his righteousness and acts unjustly, he will die for this. He will die because of the injustice he has committed. 27 But if a wicked person turns from the wickedness he has committed and does what is just and right, he will preserve his life. 28 He will certainly live because he thought it over and turned from all the transgressions he had committed; he will not die. 29 But the house of Israel says, 'The Lord's way isn't fair.' Is it my ways that are unfair, house of Israel? Instead, isn't it your ways that are unfair?

30 "Therefore, house of Israel, I will judge each one of you according to his ways." This is the declaration of the Lord God. "Repent and turn from all your rebellious acts, so they will not become a sinful stumbling block to you. 31 Throw off all the transgressions you have committed, and get yourselves a new heart and a new spirit. Why should you die, house of Israel? 32 For I take no pleasure in anyone's death." This is the declaration of the Lord God. "So repent and live!"

JOEL 2:12-13

GOD'S CALL FOR REPENTANCE

12 Even now—
   this is the Lord's declaration—
turn to me with all your heart,
with fasting, weeping, and mourning.
13 Tear your hearts,
not just your clothes,
and return to the Lord your God.
For he is gracious and compassionate,
slow to anger, abounding in faithful love,
and he relents from sending disaster.

ROMANS 2:1-11

1 Therefore, every one of you who judges is without excuse. For when you judge another, you condemn yourself, since you, the judge, do the same things. 2 Now we know that God's judgment on those who do such things is based on the truth. 3 Do you think—anyone of you who judges those who do such things yet do the same—that you will escape God's judgment? 4 Or do you despise the riches of his kindness, restraint, and patience, not recognizing that God's kindness is intended to lead you to repentance? 5 Because of your hardened and unrepentant heart you are storing up wrath for yourself in the day of wrath, when God's righteous judgment is revealed. 6 He will repay each one according to his works: 7 eternal life to those who by persistence in doing good seek glory, honor, and immortality; 8 but wrath and anger to those who are self-seeking and disobey the truth while obeying unrighteousness. 9 There will be affliction and distress for every human being who does evil, first to the Jew, and also to the Greek; 10 but glory, honor, and peace for everyone who does what is good, first to the Jew, and also to the Greek. 11 For there is no favoritism with God.

DAY 1: MATTHEW

Key Verse

From then on Jesus began to preach,
"Repent, because the kingdom of heaven
has come near."

MATTHEW 4:17

This section connects each New Testament book to the larger story of Scripture.

HOW MATTHEW FITS IN THE STORY

Our introduction to the New Testament, Matthew's Gospel contains the greatest number of direct connections to the Old Testament while also looking forward to the Messiah's future return. Matthew writes of Jesus as the climax of salvation history—the fulfillment of every prophecy and promise made to Israel, the incarnate presence and wisdom of God Himself, and the reigning sustainer of the Church.

COPY MATTHEW 4:17 INTO THE SPACE PROVIDED ON PAGE 185.

Each day features a unique question to help you connect with what you are reading.

1 How is Jesus's call to repent an invitation to follow Him?

This repeated daily question guides your reflection of how each book of the New Testament contributes to the story of redemption. (If you are feeling stuck, look for themes present in the daily reading and review the summary here on the response page for help.)

2 How does today's reading shape your understanding of the story of redemption?

RESPONSE

"For even the Son of Man did not come to be served,
but to serve, and to give his life as a ransom for many."

MARK 10:45

Gospels

Mark

WHAT IS MARK?

The Gospel of Mark is a fast-paced narrative about the ministry of Jesus. Likely written by John Mark, who knew both Peter and Paul, this Gospel emphasizes Jesus as both the Son of Man and the Son of God. It also shows Jesus as a humble servant leader, willing to suffer and die on the cross.

MARK 9:33–37

WHO IS THE GREATEST?

³³ They came to Capernaum. When he was in the house, he asked them, "What were you arguing about on the way?" ³⁴ But they were silent, because on the way they had been arguing with one another about who was the greatest. ³⁵ Sitting down, he called the Twelve and said to them, "If anyone wants to be first, he must be last and servant of all." ³⁶ He took a child, had him stand among them, and taking him in his arms, he said to them, ³⁷ "Whoever welcomes one little child such as this in my name welcomes me. And whoever welcomes me does not welcome me, but him who sent me."

MARK 10:35–45

SUFFERING AND SERVICE

³⁵ James and John, the sons of Zebedee, approached him and said, "Teacher, we want you to do whatever we ask you."

³⁶ "What do you want me to do for you?" he asked them.

³⁷ They answered him, "Allow us to sit at your right and at your left in your glory."

³⁸ Jesus said to them, "You don't know what you're asking. Are you able to drink the cup I drink or to be baptized with the baptism I am baptized with?"

³⁹ "We are able," they told him.

Jesus said to them, "You will drink the cup I drink, and you will be baptized with the baptism I am baptized with. ⁴⁰ But to sit at my right or left is not mine to give; instead, it is for those for whom it has been prepared."

⁴¹ When the ten disciples heard this, they began to be indignant with James and John. ⁴² Jesus called them over and said to them, "You know that those who are regarded as rulers of the Gentiles lord it over them, and those in high positions act as tyrants over them. ⁴³ But it is not so among you. On the contrary, whoever wants to become great among you will be your servant, ⁴⁴ and whoever wants to be first among you will be a slave to all.

⁴⁵ For even the Son of Man did not come to be served, but to serve, and to give his life as a ransom for many."

THE SERVANT'S SUFFERING AND EXALTATION

¹³ See, my servant will be successful;
he will be raised and lifted up and greatly exalted.
¹⁴ Just as many were appalled at you—
his appearance was so disfigured
that he did not look like a man,
and his form did not resemble a human being—
¹⁵ so he will sprinkle many nations.
Kings will shut their mouths because of him,
for they will see what had not been told them,
and they will understand what they had not heard.

¹ Who has believed what we have heard?
And to whom has the arm of the Lᴏʀᴅ been revealed?
² He grew up before him like a young plant
and like a root out of dry ground.
He didn't have an impressive form
or majesty that we should look at him,
no appearance that we should desire him.
³ He was despised and rejected by men,
a man of suffering who knew what sickness was.
He was like someone people turned away from;
he was despised, and we didn't value him.

⁴ Yet he himself bore our sicknesses,
and he carried our pains;
but we in turn regarded him stricken,
struck down by God, and afflicted.
⁵ But he was pierced because of our rebellion,
crushed because of our iniquities;
punishment for our peace was on him,
and we are healed by his wounds.
⁶ We all went astray like sheep;
we all have turned to our own way;
and the Lᴏʀᴅ has punished him
for the iniquity of us all.

⁷ He was oppressed and afflicted,
yet he did not open his mouth.
Like a lamb led to the slaughter
and like a sheep silent before her shearers,
he did not open his mouth.
⁸ He was taken away because of oppression and judgment,
and who considered his fate?
For he was cut off from the land of the living;
he was struck because of my people's rebellion.
⁹ He was assigned a grave with the wicked,
but he was with a rich man at his death,
because he had done no violence
and had not spoken deceitfully.

CHRIST'S HUMILITY AND EXALTATION

[5] Adopt the same attitude as that of Christ Jesus,

[6] who, existing in the form of God,
did not consider equality with God
as something to be exploited.
[7] Instead he emptied himself
by assuming the form of a servant,
taking on the likeness of humanity.
And when he had come as a man,
[8] he humbled himself by becoming obedient
to the point of death—
even to death on a cross.
[9] For this reason God highly exalted him
and gave him the name
that is above every name,
[10] so that at the name of Jesus
every knee will bow—
in heaven and on earth
and under the earth—
[11] and every tongue will confess
that Jesus Christ is Lord,
to the glory of God the Father.

DAY 2: MARK

Key Verse

"For even the Son of Man did not come to be served, but to serve, and to give his life as a ransom for many."

MARK 10:45

HOW MARK FITS IN THE STORY

The Gospel of Mark clarifies the nature of the promised Messiah. Though many individuals in Jesus's day tried to claim the title, Mark redefined it in light of Jesus's life, death, and resurrection. Jesus, the one, true Messiah, was a suffering servant, both fully human and fully divine. Mark's Gospel shows us how Jesus's authority, in both teaching and miracles, is present alongside His humanity.

COPY MARK 10:45 INTO THE SPACE PROVIDED ON PAGE 185.

1   How do today's readings about Jesus's character and demeanor change your understanding of God's posture toward His people?

2   How does today's reading shape your understanding of the story of redemption?

RESPONSE

New Testament

The Bible was written by human authors inspired by the Holy Spirit. Here are a few key facts about the authors of the New Testament.

The book of Hebrews is excluded from this extra since it does not explicitly name an author, nor does tradition hold to a commonly accepted writer.

An unexpected disciple of Jesus, Matthew the tax collector faithfully portrayed Jesus as the fulfillment of Old Testament prophecies concerning the Messiah.

LK 5:27-30

Luke was a physician and beloved co-worker of Paul. His writing provides readers with a look into Jesus's ministry, as well as the establishment of the early Church.

COL 4:14; PHM 23-24

MATTHEW

MATTHEW
1 book

LUKE · ACTS

LUKE
2 books

MARK

MARK
1 book

JOHN · 1 JOHN · 2 JOHN · 3 JOHN · REVELATION

JOHN
5 books

While not an eyewitness of Jesus's ministry, John Mark was a missionary traveling companion of Paul and Barnabas and received his account of Jesus's life from trusted eyewitnesses.

AC 13:5; 15:36-37

John was one of three disciples in Jesus's inner circle and the one Jesus entrusted to care for His mother at the cross. Through his letters, John provides a glimpse into everything from Jesus's life on earth to visions of His eventual return.

MT 4:21-22; JN 19:26-27; RV 1:1

From Pharisee and persecutor of the early Church to faithful apostle, Paul was forever changed after he encountered Jesus on the road to Damascus. He wrote thirteen of the twenty-seven books in the New Testament, helping build the Church despite imprisonment and persecution.

Timothy, Paul's son in the faith and one of his ministry partners, is listed as a co-sender of all Paul's letters except for Galatians, Romans, and 1 Corinthians. Silvanus (also known as Silas) is mentioned as a co-sender of both 1 & 2 Thessalonians, and Sosthenes is listed as a co-sender of 1 Corinthians.

AC 9:1-9, 20-22, 13:9; 2 TM 1:1

COLOSSIANS · 1 THESSALONIANS · 2 THESSALONIANS · 1 TIMOTHY · 2 TIMOTHY · TITUS · PHILEMON · ROMANS · 1 CORINTHIANS · 2 CORINTHIANS · GALATIANS · EPHESIANS · PHILIPPIANS ·

PAUL

13 books

Growing up as Jesus's brother, James did not believe Jesus was the Son of God until after His resurrection. James went on to lead the Jerusalem church and played a key role in the Jerusalem Council, developing language around the Gentile relationship to the Jewish law.

MK 6:3; AC 15:13-21; 1CO 15:7; JMS 1:1

JAMES

JAMES

1 book

1 PETER · 2 PETER

PETER

2 books

JUDE

JUDE

1 book

While sometimes known as the disciple who denied Jesus, Peter, a former fisherman, was a faithful follower of Christ who led many to faith as he helped establish the early Church.

MT 16:13-19; LK 22:54-61; JN 21:15-19; AC 2:14-41

While less is known about Jude (most likely the brother of Jesus, also known as Judas), he used his epistle to urge its recipients to protect Christian truth against heresy and false teachers.

MT 13:55; JD 1

Luke

WHAT IS LUKE?

This Gospel was written by Luke, a physician and coworker of the apostle Paul. It is a detailed account of the life and ministry of Jesus. Luke places special emphasis on Jesus's concern for including social outsiders and seeking the lost. Luke is the longest book in the New Testament and contains many stories and teachings found only in this Gospel.

LUKE 15:1–7
THE PARABLE OF THE LOST SHEEP

¹ All the tax collectors and sinners were approaching to listen to him. ² And the Pharisees and scribes were complaining, "This man welcomes sinners and eats with them."

³ So he told them this parable: ⁴ "What man among you, who has a hundred sheep and loses one of them, does not leave the ninety-nine in the open field and go after the lost one until he finds it? ⁵ When he has found it, he joyfully puts it on his shoulders, ⁶ and coming home, he calls his friends and neighbors together, saying to them, 'Rejoice with me, because I have found my lost sheep!' ⁷ I tell you, in the same way, there will be more joy in heaven over one sinner who repents than over ninety-nine righteous people who don't need repentance."

LUKE 19:1–10
JESUS VISITS ZACCHAEUS

¹ He entered Jericho and was passing through. ² There was a man named Zacchaeus who was a chief tax collector, and he

was rich. ³ He was trying to see who Jesus was, but he was not able because of the crowd, since he was a short man. ⁴ So running ahead, he climbed up a sycamore tree to see Jesus, since he was about to pass that way. ⁵ When Jesus came to the place, he looked up and said to him, "Zacchaeus, hurry and come down because today it is necessary for me to stay at your house."

⁶ So he quickly came down and welcomed him joyfully. ⁷ All who saw it began to complain, "He's gone to stay with a sinful man."

⁸ But Zacchaeus stood there and said to the Lord, "Look, I'll give half of my possessions to the poor, Lord. And if I have extorted anything from anyone, I'll pay back four times as much."

⁹ "Today salvation has come to this house," Jesus told him, "because he too is a son of Abraham.

KEY VERSE

¹⁰ For the Son of Man has come to seek and to save the lost."

JEREMIAH 50:6-7, 17-20

⁶ "My people were lost sheep;
their shepherds led them astray,
guiding them the wrong way in the mountains.
They wandered from mountain to hill;
they forgot their resting place.
⁷ Whoever found them devoured them.
Their adversaries said, 'We're not guilty;
instead, they have sinned against the LORD,
their righteous grazing land,
the hope of their ancestors, the LORD.'"

…

THE RETURN OF GOD'S PEOPLE

¹⁷ "Israel is a stray lamb, chased by lions.
The first who devoured him was the king of Assyria;
the last who crushed his bones
was King Nebuchadnezzar of Babylon.

¹⁸ Therefore, this is what the LORD of Armies, the God of Israel, says: I am about to punish the king of Babylon and his land just as I punished the king of Assyria.

¹⁹ I will return Israel to his grazing land,
and he will feed on Carmel and Bashan;
he will be satisfied
in the hill country of Ephraim and of Gilead.
²⁰ In those days and at that time—
   this is the LORD's declaration—
one will search for Israel's iniquity,
but there will be none,
and for Judah's sins,
but they will not be found,
for I will forgive those I leave as a remnant."

EZEKIEL 34:11-16

¹¹ "For this is what the Lord GOD says: See, I myself will search for my flock and look for them. ¹² As a shepherd looks for his sheep on the day he is among his scattered flock, so I will look for my flock. I will rescue them from all the places where they have been scattered on a day of clouds and total darkness. ¹³ I will bring them out from the peoples, gather them from the countries, and bring them to their own soil. I will shepherd them on the mountains of Israel, in the ravines, and in all the inhabited places of the land. ¹⁴ I will tend them in good pasture, and their grazing place will be on Israel's lofty mountains. There they will lie down in a good grazing place; they will feed in rich pasture on the mountains of Israel. ¹⁵ I will tend my flock and let them lie down. This is the declaration of the Lord GOD. ¹⁶ I will seek the lost, bring back the strays, bandage the injured, and strengthen the weak, but I will destroy the fat and the strong. I will shepherd them with justice."

EPHESIANS 1:7-8

⁷ In him we have redemption through his blood, the forgiveness of our trespasses, according to the riches of his grace ⁸ that he richly poured out on us with all wisdom and understanding.

Key Verse

"For the Son of Man has come to seek and to save the lost."

LUKE 19:10

HOW LUKE FITS IN THE STORY

Luke's Gospel has a unique focus on Jesus as a friend of sinners and Savior of the world. In focusing on Jesus as the Son of Man who came to seek and save the lost, this Gospel pays close attention to how Jesus engaged with the marginalized. It also highlights His conversations with the religious leaders of the day, as well as His teachings on the nature of the kingdom of God. Luke shows how salvation, predicted by the Old Testament prophets, has arrived in Jesus and is available to the whole world.

COPY LUKE 19:10 INTO THE SPACE PROVIDED ON PAGE 185.

1 How does Luke 19:1–10 clarify your understanding of Jesus's mission on earth?

2 How does today's reading shape your understanding of the story of redemption?

RESPONSE

John

WHAT IS JOHN?

About 90 percent of the material in the Gospel of John is unique to this book of the Bible. John, a disciple of Jesus, highlighted Jesus's identity as the Son who reveals the nature of God the Father. He also points to how Jesus fulfills Old Testament prophecy, festivals, and institutions.

JOHN 1:1-18

KEY VERSE

¹ In the beginning was the Word, and the Word was with God, and the Word was God.

² He was with God in the beginning. ³ All things were created through him, and apart from him not one thing was created that has been created. ⁴ In him was life, and that life was the light of men. ⁵ That light shines in the darkness, and yet the darkness did not overcome it.

⁶ There was a man sent from God whose name was John. ⁷ He came as a witness to testify about the light, so that all might believe through him. ⁸ He was not the light, but he came to testify about the light. ⁹ The true light that gives light to everyone was coming into the world.

¹⁰ He was in the world, and the world was created through him, and yet the world did not recognize him. ¹¹ He came to his own, and his own people did not receive him. ¹² But to all who did receive him, he gave them the right to be children of God, to those who believe in his name, ¹³ who were born, not of natural descent, or of the will of the flesh, or of the will of man, but of God.

¹⁴ The Word became flesh and dwelt among us. We observed his glory, the glory as the one and only Son from the Father, full of grace and truth. ¹⁵ (John testified concerning him and exclaimed, "This was the one of whom I said, 'The one coming after me ranks ahead of me, because he existed before me.'") ¹⁶ Indeed, we have all received grace upon grace from his fullness, ¹⁷ for the law was given through Moses; grace and truth came through Jesus Christ. ¹⁸ No one has ever seen God. The one and only Son, who is himself God and is at the Father's side—he has revealed him.

JOHN 5:17-23

HONORING THE FATHER AND THE SON

¹⁷ Jesus responded to them, "My Father is still working, and I am working also." ¹⁸ This is why the Jews began trying all the

more to kill him: Not only was he breaking the Sabbath, but he was even calling God his own Father, making himself equal to God.

[19] Jesus replied, "Truly I tell you, the Son is not able to do anything on his own, but only what he sees the Father doing. For whatever the Father does, the Son likewise does these things. [20] For the Father loves the Son and shows him everything he is doing, and he will show him greater works than these so that you will be amazed. [21] And just as the Father raises the dead and gives them life, so the Son also gives life to whom he wants. [22] The Father, in fact, judges no one but has given all judgment to the Son, [23] so that all people may honor the Son just as they honor the Father. Anyone who does not honor the Son does not honor the Father who sent him."

GENESIS 1:1-5

[1] In the beginning God created the heavens and the earth. [2] Now the earth was formless and empty, darkness covered the surface of the watery depths, and the Spirit of God was hovering over the surface of the waters. [3] Then God said, "Let there be light," and there was light. [4] God saw that the light was good, and God separated the light from the darkness. [5] God called the light "day," and the darkness he called "night." There was an evening, and there was a morning: one day.

REVELATION 1:4-8

[4] John: To the seven churches in Asia. Grace and peace to you from the one who is, who was, and who is to come, and from the seven spirits before his throne, [5] and from Jesus Christ, the faithful witness, the firstborn from the dead and the ruler of the kings of the earth.

To him who loves us and has set us free from our sins by his blood, [6] and made us a kingdom, priests to his God and Father—to him be glory and dominion forever and ever. Amen.

[7] Look, he is coming with the clouds,
and every eye will see him,
even those who pierced him.
And all the tribes of the earth
will mourn over him.
So it is to be. Amen.

[8] "I am the Alpha and the Omega," says the Lord God, "the one who is, who was, and who is to come, the Almighty."

Key Verse

In the beginning was the Word,
and the Word was with God, and
the Word was God.

JOHN 1:1

HOW JOHN FITS IN THE STORY

Of all the New Testament books, the Gospel of John most clearly teaches the divine identity of Christ. Rather than focusing on the miracles, parables, and public speeches that are so prominent in the other Gospel accounts, John emphasizes the identity of Jesus as the Son of God and His invitation to respond in faith.

COPY JOHN 1:1 INTO THE SPACE PROVIDED ON PAGE 185.

1   How does Jesus describe His relationship to God the Father in today's reading? How do these passages broaden or change your understanding of who Jesus is?

2   How does today's reading shape your understanding of the story of redemption?

RESPONSE

Church History

Acts

WHAT IS ACTS?

The book of Acts is the second volume written by Luke. It continues where the Gospel of Luke ends, recording the work of the early apostles to spread the gospel in Jerusalem and the greater Mediterranean world. This historical account also documents how the early Church was built—person by person in city after city—through the dynamic power of the Holy Spirit.

ACTS 1:4–11
THE HOLY SPIRIT PROMISED

⁴ While he was with them, he commanded them not to leave Jerusalem, but to wait for the Father's promise. "Which," he said, "you have heard me speak about; ⁵ for John baptized with water, but you will be baptized with the Holy Spirit in a few days."

⁶ So when they had come together, they asked him, "Lord, are you restoring the kingdom to Israel at this time?"

⁷ He said to them, "It is not for you to know times or periods that the Father has set by his own authority.

⁸ But you will receive power when the Holy Spirit has come on you, and you will be my witnesses in Jerusalem, in all Judea and Samaria, and to the ends of the earth."

KEY VERSE

THE ASCENSION

⁹ After he had said this, he was taken up as they were watching, and a cloud took him out of their sight. ¹⁰ While he was going, they were gazing into heaven, and suddenly two men in white clothes stood by them. ¹¹ They said, "Men of Galilee, why do you stand looking up into heaven? This same Jesus, who has been taken from you into heaven, will come in the same way that you have seen him going into heaven."

ACTS 2:1–13
PENTECOST

¹ When the day of Pentecost had arrived, they were all together in one place. ² Suddenly a sound like that of a violent rushing wind came from heaven, and it filled the whole house where they were staying. ³ They saw tongues like flames of fire that separated and rested on each one of them. ⁴ Then they were all filled with the Holy Spirit and began to speak in different tongues, as the Spirit enabled them.

⁵ Now there were Jews staying in Jerusalem, devout people from every nation under heaven. ⁶ When this sound occurred, a crowd came together and was confused because each one heard them speaking in his own language. ⁷ They were astounded and amazed, saying, "Look, aren't all these who are speaking Galileans? ⁸ How is it that each of us can hear them in our own native language? ⁹ Parthians, Medes, Elamites; those who live in Mesopotamia, in Judea and Cappadocia, Pontus and Asia, ¹⁰ Phrygia and Pamphylia, Egypt and the parts of Libya near Cyrene; visitors from Rome (both Jews and converts), ¹¹ Cretans and Arabs—we hear them declaring the magnificent acts of God in our own tongues." ¹² They were all astounded and perplexed, saying to one another, "What does this mean?" ¹³ But some sneered and said, "They're drunk on new wine."

JOEL 2:28-32
GOD'S PROMISE OF HIS SPIRIT

²⁸ "After this
I will pour out my Spirit on all humanity;
then your sons and your daughters will prophesy,
your old men will have dreams,
and your young men will see visions.
²⁹ I will even pour out my Spirit
on the male and female slaves in those days.
³⁰ I will display wonders
in the heavens and on the earth:
blood, fire, and columns of smoke.
³¹ The sun will be turned to darkness
and the moon to blood
before the great and terrible day of the LORD comes.
³² Then everyone who calls
on the name of the LORD will be saved,
for there will be an escape
for those on Mount Zion and in Jerusalem,
as the LORD promised,
among the survivors the LORD calls."

JOHN 14:15-31
ANOTHER COUNSELOR PROMISED

¹⁵ "If you love me, you will keep my commands. ¹⁶ And I will ask the Father, and he will give you another Counselor to be with you forever. ¹⁷ He is the Spirit of truth. The world is unable to receive him because it doesn't see him or know him. But you do know him, because he remains with you and will be in you.

[18] "I will not leave you as orphans; I am coming to you. [19] In a little while the world will no longer see me, but you will see me. Because I live, you will live too. [20] On that day you will know that I am in my Father, you are in me, and I am in you. [21] The one who has my commands and keeps them is the one who loves me. And the one who loves me will be loved by my Father. I also will love him and will reveal myself to him."

[22] Judas (not Iscariot) said to him, "Lord, how is it you're going to reveal yourself to us and not to the world?"

[23] Jesus answered, "If anyone loves me, he will keep my word. My Father will love him, and we will come to him and make our home with him. [24] The one who doesn't love me will not keep my words. The word that you hear is not mine but is from the Father who sent me.

[25] "I have spoken these things to you while I remain with you. [26] But the Counselor, the Holy Spirit, whom the Father will send in my name, will teach you all things and remind you of everything I have told you.

JESUS'S GIFT OF PEACE

[27] "Peace I leave with you. My peace I give to you. I do not give to you as the world gives. Don't let your heart be troubled or fearful. [28] You have heard me tell you, 'I am going away and I am coming to you.' If you loved me, you would rejoice that I am going to the Father, because the Father is greater than I. [29] I have told you now before it happens so that when it does happen you may believe. [30] I will not talk with you much longer, because the ruler of the world is coming. He has no power over me. [31] On the contrary, so that the world may know that I love the Father, I do as the Father commanded me.

"Get up; let's leave this place."

Key Verse

"But you will receive power when the Holy Spirit has come on you, and you will be my witnesses in Jerusalem, in all Judea and Samaria, and to the ends of the earth."

ACTS 1:8

HOW ACTS FITS IN THE STORY

The book of Acts bridges the years between those who walked with Jesus firsthand and those who came to faith through their testimony. This book shows the fulfillment of Jesus's promise to send the Holy Spirit to His disciples, and how the Holy Spirit sustained, equipped, and grew the early Church. It also gives us context for much of the New Testament, especially Paul's letters to the churches he helped establish during his missionary journeys.

COPY ACTS 1:8 INTO THE SPACE PROVIDED ON PAGE 185.

1 According to Acts 1:8, what is one purpose of the Holy Spirit? How does today's reading expand your understanding of who the Holy Spirit is?

2 How does today's reading shape your understanding of the story of redemption?

RESPONSE

DAY 6

GRACE DAY

Take this day to catch up on your reading,
pray, and rest in the presence of the Lord.

Tear your hearts, not just
your clothes, and return to
the LORD your God. For he is
gracious and compassionate,
slow to anger, abounding in
faithful love, and he relents
from sending disaster.

JOEL 2:13

DAY 7

WEEKLY TRUTH

As we look at the New Testament together, we'll commit Acts 13:27–31 to memory. In the second half of this sermon from Acts 13, Paul speaks about the role Israel played in Christ's death, fulfilling Old Testament prophecies about a coming Savior. This passage reminds us that, as believers, we serve the risen Lord while bearing witness to the hope of the gospel.

This week, let's begin our memorization with just the first verse of this passage. To help you visualize what's being described in the text, underline the subject of verse 27, circle who or what they didn't recognize, and draw a square around what happened as a result.

Since the residents of Jerusalem and their rulers did not recognize him or the sayings of the prophets that are read every Sabbath, they have fulfilled their words by condemning him.

ACTS 13:27

For all have sinned and fall short of the glory of God; they are justified freely by his grace through the redemption that is in Christ Jesus.

ROMANS 3:23–24

Pauline Epistles

Romans

WHAT IS ROMANS?

Romans is a letter written by Paul to Jewish and Gentile Christians in Rome. In it, Paul offers clarity on the source of salvation and righteousness, and he encourages unity among Christians from all backgrounds.

ROMANS 2:17–24

17 Now if you call yourself a Jew, and rely on the law, and boast in God, 18 and know his will, and approve the things that are superior, being instructed from the law, 19 and if you are convinced that you are a guide for the blind, a light to those in darkness, 20 an instructor of the ignorant, a teacher of the immature, having the embodiment of knowledge and truth in the law— 21 you then, who teach another, don't you teach yourself? You who preach, "You must not steal"—do you steal? 22 You who say, "You must not commit adultery"—do you commit adultery? You who detest idols, do you rob temples? 23 You who boast in the law, do you dishonor God by breaking the law? 24 For, as it is written: The name of God is blasphemed among the Gentiles because of you.

ROMANS 3:9–26
THE WHOLE WORLD GUILTY BEFORE GOD

9 What then? Are we any better off? Not at all! For we have already charged that both Jews and Greeks are all under sin, 10 as it is written:

There is no one righteous, not even one.
[11] There is no one who understands;
there is no one who seeks God.
[12] All have turned away;
all alike have become worthless.
There is no one who does what is good,
not even one.
[13] Their throat is an open grave;
they deceive with their tongues.
Vipers' venom is under their lips.
[14] Their mouth is full of cursing and bitterness.
[15] Their feet are swift to shed blood;
[16] ruin and wretchedness are in their paths,
[17] and the path of peace they have not known.
[18] There is no fear of God before their eyes.

[19] Now we know that whatever the law says, it speaks to those who are subject to the law, so that every mouth may be shut and the whole world may become subject to God's judgment. [20] For no one will be justified in his sight by the works of the law, because the knowledge of sin comes through the law.

THE RIGHTEOUSNESS OF GOD THROUGH FAITH

[21] But now, apart from the law, the righteousness of God has been revealed, attested by the Law and the Prophets. [22] The righteousness of God is through faith in Jesus Christ, since there is no distinction.

[23] For all have sinned and fall short of the glory of God; [24] they are justified freely by his grace through the redemption that is in Christ Jesus.

[25] God presented him as the mercy seat by his blood, through faith, to demonstrate his righteousness, because in his restraint God passed over the sins previously committed. [26] God presented him to demonstrate his righteousness at the present time, so that he would be just and justify the one who has faith in Jesus.

ROMANS 5:1–11

[1] Therefore, since we have been justified by faith, we have peace with God through our Lord Jesus Christ. [2] We have also obtained access through him by faith into this grace in

which we stand, and we boast in the hope of the glory of God. [3] And not only that, but we also boast in our afflictions, because we know that affliction produces endurance, [4] endurance produces proven character, and proven character produces hope. [5] This hope will not disappoint us, because God's love has been poured out in our hearts through the Holy Spirit who was given to us.

THE JUSTIFIED ARE RECONCILED

[6] For while we were still helpless, at the right time, Christ died for the ungodly. [7] For rarely will someone die for a just person—though for a good person perhaps someone might even dare to die. [8] But God proves his own love for us in that while we were still sinners, Christ died for us. [9] How much more then, since we have now been justified by his blood, will we be saved through him from wrath. [10] For if, while we were enemies, we were reconciled to God through the death of his Son, then how much more, having been reconciled, will we be saved by his life. [11] And not only that, but we also boast in God through our Lord Jesus Christ, through whom we have now received this reconciliation.

PSALM 14:1–3
A PORTRAIT OF SINNERS

For the choir director. Of David.

[1] The fool says in his heart, "There's no God."
They are corrupt; they do vile deeds.
There is no one who does good.
[2] The LORD looks down from heaven on the human race
to see if there is one who is wise,
one who seeks God.
[3] All have turned away;
all alike have become corrupt.
There is no one who does good,
not even one.

ISAIAH 59:14–20
[14] Justice is turned back,
and righteousness stands far off.
For truth has stumbled in the public square,
and honesty cannot enter.
[15] Truth is missing,

KEY VERSE

and whoever turns from evil is plundered.
The Lord saw that there was no justice,
and he was offended.
[16] He saw that there was no man—
he was amazed that there was no one interceding;
so his own arm brought salvation,
and his own righteousness supported him.

[17] He put on righteousness as body armor,
and a helmet of salvation on his head;
he put on garments of vengeance for clothing,
and he wrapped himself in zeal as in a cloak.
[18] So he will repay according to their deeds:
fury to his enemies,
retribution to his foes,
and he will repay the coasts and islands.
[19] They will fear the name of the Lord in the west
and his glory in the east;
for he will come like a rushing stream
driven by the wind of the Lord.
[20] "The Redeemer will come to Zion,
and to those in Jacob who turn from transgression."
   This is the Lord's declaration.

Key Verse

For all have sinned and fall short of the glory of God; they are justified freely by his grace through the redemption that is in Christ Jesus.

ROMANS 3:23–24

HOW ROMANS FITS IN THE STORY

The book of Romans highlights the effect of sin on all of creation. Romans includes a detailed explanation, unlike any other in the Bible, for why righteousness can only come through grace by faith in Jesus Christ. It also emphasizes the power of the cross and how it changes us—from sinners worthy of God's punishment to His beloved children—and calls us to live in eager anticipation of Jesus's return.

COPY ROMANS 3:23–24 INTO THE SPACE PROVIDED ON PAGE 185.

1 After reading today's passages, how would you describe the difference between unrighteousness and God's righteousness?

2 How does today's reading shape your understanding of the story of redemption?

54   THIS IS THE NEW TESTAMENT

RESPONSE

1 Corinthians

WHAT IS 1 CORINTHIANS?

First Corinthians is a letter written by Paul to the church in Corinth. The Corinthian church was struggling to stay faithful to the gospel while living as a part of the larger, non-Christian Corinthian culture. With this in mind, Paul gave practical instruction on love and Christian unity, spiritual gifts and marriage, resurrection and the life of the Church.

1 CORINTHIANS 1:4–9
THANKSGIVING

⁴ I always thank my God for you because of the grace of God given to you in Christ Jesus, ⁵ that you were enriched in him in every way, in all speech and all knowledge. ⁶ In this way, the testimony about Christ was confirmed among you, ⁷ so that you do not lack any spiritual gift as you eagerly wait for the revelation of our Lord Jesus Christ. ⁸ He will also strengthen you to the end, so that you will be blameless in the day of our Lord Jesus Christ.

▶ KEY VERSE

⁹ God is faithful; you were called by him into fellowship with his Son, Jesus Christ our Lord.

1 CORINTHIANS 10:16–17

¹⁶ The cup of blessing that we bless, is it not a sharing in the blood of Christ? The bread that we break, is it not a sharing in the body of Christ? ¹⁷ Because there is one bread, we who are many are one body, since all of us share the one bread.

1 CORINTHIANS 12:12–31
UNITY YET DIVERSITY IN THE BODY

¹² For just as the body is one and has many parts, and all the parts of that body, though many, are one body—so also is Christ. ¹³ For we were all baptized by one Spirit into one body—whether Jews or Greeks, whether slaves or free—and we were all given one Spirit to drink. ¹⁴ Indeed, the body is not one part but many. ¹⁵ If the foot should say, "Because I'm not a hand, I don't belong to the body," it is not for that reason any less a part of the body. ¹⁶ And if the ear should say, "Because I'm not an eye, I don't belong to the body," it is not for that reason any less a part of the body. ¹⁷ If the whole body were an eye, where would the hearing be? If the whole body were an ear, where would the sense of smell be? ¹⁸ But as it is, God has arranged each one of the parts in the body just as he wanted. ¹⁹ And if they were all the same part, where would the body be? ²⁰ As it is, there are many parts, but one body. ²¹ The eye cannot say to the hand, "I don't need you!" Or again, the head can't say to the feet, "I don't need you!" ²² On the contrary, those parts of the body that are weaker

are indispensable. [23] And those parts of the body that we consider less honorable, we clothe these with greater honor, and our unrespectable parts are treated with greater respect, [24] which our respectable parts do not need.

Instead, God has put the body together, giving greater honor to the less honorable, [25] so that there would be no division in the body, but that the members would have the same concern for each other. [26] So if one member suffers, all the members suffer with it; if one member is honored, all the members rejoice with it.

[27] Now you are the body of Christ, and individual members of it. [28] And God has appointed these in the church: first apostles, second prophets, third teachers, next miracles, then gifts of healing, helping, leading, various kinds of tongues. [29] Are all apostles? Are all prophets? Are all teachers? Do all do miracles? [30] Do all have gifts of healing? Do all speak in tongues? Do all interpret? [31] But desire the greater gifts. And I will show you an even better way.

EXODUS 19:5–6

[5] "'Now if you will carefully listen to me and keep my covenant, you will be my own possession out of all the peoples, although the whole earth is mine, [6] and you will be my kingdom of priests and my holy nation.' These are the words that you are to say to the Israelites."

JEREMIAH 7:21–23

[21] This is what the LORD of Armies, the God of Israel, says: "Add your burnt offerings to your other sacrifices, and eat the meat yourselves, [22] for when I brought your ancestors out of the land of Egypt, I did not speak with them or command them concerning burnt offering and sacrifice. [23] However, I did give them this command: 'Obey me, and then I will be your God, and you will be my people. Follow every way I command you so that it may go well with you.'"

Key Verse

God is faithful; you were called by him into fellowship with his Son, Jesus Christ our Lord.

1 CORINTHIANS 1:9

HOW 1 CORINTHIANS FITS IN THE STORY

First Corinthians contributes greatly to our understanding of Christian life, ministry, and relationships by showing us how the members of the Church—called the body of Christ—are to function together. Paul gave specific solutions to specific problems the Corinthian church faced. Yet the underlying answer to every question is the call to live Christ-centered lives in community, no matter the culture or circumstance.

COPY 1 CORINTHIANS 1:9 INTO THE SPACE PROVIDED ON PAGE 186.

1   How has God called you into fellowship with our Lord, Jesus Christ? How does that fellowship connect you to other believers in the Church?

2   How does today's reading shape your understanding of the story of redemption?

RESPONSE

2 Corinthians

WHAT IS 2 CORINTHIANS?

Second Corinthians was written during Paul's third missionary journey. In his second letter to the Corinthian church, Paul defends his ministry as an apostle and describes how Satan has opposed the work of the gospel. He also expresses his joy over the church's restoration after troubling conflict.

2 CORINTHIANS 4:1–12
THE LIGHT OF THE GOSPEL

[1] Therefore, since we have this ministry because we were shown mercy, we do not give up. [2] Instead, we have renounced secret and shameful things, not acting deceitfully or distorting the word of God, but commending ourselves before God to everyone's conscience by an open display of the truth. [3] But if our gospel is veiled, it is veiled to those who are perishing. [4] In their case, the god of this age has blinded the minds of the unbelievers to keep them from seeing the light of the gospel of the glory of Christ, who is the image of God. [5] For we are not proclaiming ourselves but Jesus Christ as Lord, and ourselves as your servants for Jesus's sake. [6] For God who said, "Let light shine out of darkness," has shone in our hearts to give the light of the knowledge of God's glory in the face of Jesus Christ.

TREASURE IN CLAY JARS

[7] Now we have this treasure in clay jars, so that this extraordinary power may be from God and not from us. [8] We

are afflicted in every way but not crushed; we are perplexed but not in despair; [9] we are persecuted but not abandoned; we are struck down but not destroyed. [10] We always carry the death of Jesus in our body, so that the life of Jesus may also be displayed in our body. [11] For we who live are always being given over to death for Jesus's sake, so that Jesus's life may also be displayed in our mortal flesh. [12] So then, death is at work in us, but life in you.

2 CORINTHIANS 12:1–10
SUFFICIENT GRACE

[1] Boasting is necessary. It is not profitable, but I will move on to visions and revelations of the Lord. [2] I know a man in Christ who was caught up to the third heaven fourteen years ago. Whether he was in the body or out of the body, I don't know; God knows. [3] I know that this man—whether in the body or out of the body I don't know; God knows— [4] was caught up into paradise and heard inexpressible words, which a human being is not allowed to speak. [5] I will boast about this person, but not about myself, except of my weaknesses.

[6] For if I want to boast, I wouldn't be a fool, because I would be telling the truth. But I will spare you, so that no one can credit me with something beyond what he sees in me or hears from me, [7] especially because of the extraordinary revelations. Therefore, so that I would not exalt myself, a thorn in the flesh was given to me, a messenger of Satan to torment me so that I would not exalt myself. [8] Concerning this, I pleaded with the Lord three times that it would leave me.

KEY VERSE

[9] But he said to me, "My grace is sufficient for you, for my power is perfected in weakness."

Therefore, I will most gladly boast all the more about my weaknesses, so that Christ's power may reside in me.

[10] So I take pleasure in weaknesses, insults, hardships, persecutions, and in difficulties, for the sake of Christ. For when I am weak, then I am strong.

PSALM 27:1–3
MY STRONGHOLD

Of David.

[1] The LORD is my light and my salvation—
whom should I fear?
The LORD is the stronghold of my life—
whom should I dread?
[2] When evildoers came against me to devour my flesh,
my foes and my enemies stumbled and fell.
[3] Though an army deploys against me,
my heart will not be afraid;
though a war breaks out against me,
I will still be confident.

DANIEL 10:19

He said, "Don't be afraid, you who are treasured by God. Peace to you; be very strong!"

As he spoke to me, I was strengthened and said, "Let my lord speak, for you have strengthened me."

EPHESIANS 6:12–18

[12] For our struggle is not against flesh and blood, but against the rulers, against the authorities, against the cosmic powers of this darkness, against evil, spiritual forces in the heavens. [13] For this reason take up the full armor of God, so that you may be able to resist in the evil day, and having prepared everything, to take your stand. [14] Stand, therefore, with truth like a belt around your waist, righteousness like armor on your chest, [15] and your feet sandaled with readiness for the gospel of peace. [16] In every situation take up the shield of faith with which you can extinguish all the flaming arrows of the evil one. [17] Take the helmet of salvation and the sword of the Spirit—which is the word of God. [18] Pray at all times in the Spirit with every prayer and request, and stay alert with all perseverance and intercession for all the saints.

Key Verse

But he said to me, "My grace is sufficient for you, for my power is perfected in weakness." Therefore, I will most gladly boast all the more about my weaknesses, so that Christ's power may reside in me.

2 CORINTHIANS 12:9

HOW 2 CORINTHIANS FITS IN THE STORY

Second Corinthians contains some of Paul's most direct teaching about his role as a pastor. This letter gives a biblical understanding of ministry, the work of God's people. It explains that God is reconciling the world to Himself in Christ, and we are invited to participate in this ongoing act of reconciliation. It also teaches that true ministry in Christ's name will encounter opposition and suffering, as well as victory.

COPY 2 CORINTHIANS 12:9 INTO THE SPACE PROVIDED ON PAGE 186.

1 What does Paul mean when he says God's power is made perfect in weakness? In what ways has God's strength been demonstrated through your own weaknesses?

2 How does today's reading shape your understanding of the story of redemption?

RESPONSE

Pauline Epistles

Galatians

WHAT IS GALATIANS?

Galatians is a letter written by Paul to churches in Galatia to clearly communicate the gospel message. He writes that sinners can be justified, or moved from a state of sin to a state of righteousness, through faith in Jesus Christ. This faith, rather than obedience to the law, is what leads to godly living.

GALATIANS 2:15–21
FREEDOM FROM THE LAW

[15] We are Jews by birth and not "Gentile sinners," [16] and yet because we know that a person is not justified by the works of the law but by faith in Jesus Christ, even we ourselves have believed in Christ Jesus. This was so that we might be justified by faith in Christ and not by the works of the law, because by the works of the law no human being will be justified. [17] But if we ourselves are also found to be "sinners" while seeking to be justified by Christ, is Christ then a promoter of sin? Absolutely not! [18] If I rebuild those things that I tore down, I show myself to be a lawbreaker. [19] For through the law I died to the law, so that I might live for God. [20] I have been crucified with Christ, and I no longer live, but Christ lives in me. The life I now live in the body, I live by faith in the Son of God, who loved me and gave himself for me.

KEY VERSE

[21] I do not set aside the grace of God, for if righteousness comes through the law, then Christ died for nothing.

THE PURPOSE OF THE LAW

[19] Why, then, was the law given? It was added for the sake of transgressions until the Seed to whom the promise was made would come. The law was put into effect through angels by means of a mediator. [20] Now a mediator is not just for one person alone, but God is one. [21] Is the law therefore contrary to God's promises? Absolutely not! For if the law had been granted with the ability to give life, then righteousness would certainly be on the basis of the law. [22] But the Scripture imprisoned everything under sin's power, so that the promise might be given on the basis of faith in Jesus Christ to those who believe. [23] Before this faith came, we were confined under the law, imprisoned until the coming faith was revealed. [24] The law, then, was our guardian until Christ, so that we could be justified by faith. [25] But since that faith has come, we are no longer under a guardian, [26] for through faith you are all sons of God in Christ Jesus.

SONS AND HEIRS

[27] For those of you who were baptized into Christ have been clothed with Christ. [28] There is no Jew or Greek, slave or free, male and female; since you are all one in Christ Jesus. [29] And if you belong to Christ, then you are Abraham's seed, heirs according to the promise.

[1] Now I say that as long as the heir is a child, he differs in no way from a slave, though he is the owner of everything. [2] Instead, he is under guardians and trustees until the time set by his father. [3] In the same way we also, when we were children, were in slavery under the elements of the world. [4] When the time came to completion, God sent his Son, born of a woman, born under the law, [5] to redeem those under the law, so that we might receive adoption as sons. [6] And because you are sons, God sent the Spirit of his Son into our hearts, crying, *"Abba,* Father!" [7] So you are no longer a slave but a son, and if a son, then God has made you an heir.

FREEDOM OF THE CHRISTIAN

[1] For freedom, Christ set us free. Stand firm, then, and don't submit again to a yoke of slavery.

…

[13] For you were called to be free, brothers and sisters; only don't use this freedom as an opportunity for the flesh, but serve one another through love. [14] For the whole law is fulfilled in one statement: Love your neighbor as yourself. [15] But if you bite and devour one another, watch out, or you will be consumed by one another.

THE SPIRIT VERSUS THE FLESH

[16] I say, then, walk by the Spirit and you will certainly not carry out the desire of the flesh. [17] For the flesh desires what is against the Spirit, and the Spirit desires what is against the flesh; these are opposed to each other, so that you don't do what you want. [18] But if you are led by the Spirit, you are not under the law.

[19] Now the works of the flesh are obvious: sexual immorality, moral impurity, promiscuity, [20] idolatry, sorcery, hatreds, strife, jealousy, outbursts of anger, selfish ambitions, dissensions, factions, [21] envy, drunkenness, carousing, and anything similar. I am warning you about these things—as I warned you before—that those who practice such things will not inherit the kingdom of God.

[22] But the fruit of the Spirit is love, joy, peace, patience, kindness, goodness, faithfulness, [23] gentleness, and self-control. The law is not against such things. [24] Now those who belong to Christ Jesus have crucified the flesh with its passions and desires. [25] If we live by the Spirit, let us also keep in step with the Spirit.

THE ABRAHAMIC COVENANT

[1] After these events, the word of the LORD came to Abram in a vision:

Do not be afraid, Abram.
I am your shield;

your reward will be very great.

[2] But Abram said, "Lord GOD, what can you give me, since I am childless and the heir of my house is Eliezer of Damascus?" [3] Abram continued, "Look, you have given me no offspring, so a slave born in my house will be my heir."

[4] Now the word of the LORD came to him: "This one will not be your heir; instead, one who comes from your own body will be your heir." [5] He took him outside and said, "Look at the sky and count the stars, if you are able to count them." Then he said to him, "Your offspring will be that numerous."

[6] Abram believed the LORD, and he credited it to him as righteousness.

GENESIS 22:15-18

[15] Then the angel of the LORD called to Abraham a second time from heaven [16] and said, "By myself I have sworn," this is the LORD's declaration: "Because you have done this thing and have not withheld your only son, [17] I will indeed bless you and make your offspring as numerous as the stars of the sky and the sand on the seashore. Your offspring will possess the city gates of their enemies. [18] And all the nations of the earth will be blessed by your offspring because you have obeyed my command."

ROMANS 10:1-4
RIGHTEOUSNESS BY FAITH ALONE

[1] Brothers and sisters, my heart's desire and prayer to God concerning them is for their salvation. [2] I can testify about them that they have zeal for God, but not according to knowledge. [3] Since they are ignorant of the righteousness of God and attempted to establish their own righteousness, they have not submitted to God's righteousness. [4] For Christ is the end of the law for righteousness to everyone who believes.

Key Verse

I do not set aside the grace of God, for if righteousness comes through the law, then Christ died for nothing.

GALATIANS 2:21

HOW GALATIANS FITS IN THE STORY

In Galatians, we find a summary of the true gospel: salvation comes through faith in Jesus Christ alone and not the law. In this letter, Paul teaches extensively about the ongoing work of the Holy Spirit in the Christian life, including commands to "walk by the Spirit," "be led by the Spirit," and to "keep in step with the Spirit." This submission to the Holy Spirit in every moment is what empowers us to live godly lives and carry out the work of the gospel.

COPY GALATIANS 2:21 INTO THE SPACE PROVIDED ON PAGE 186.

1 What does today's reading from Galatians say about living by faith?

2 How does today's reading shape your understanding of the story of redemption?

For you are saved by grace through faith, and this is not from yourselves;
it is God's gift—not from works, so that no one can boast.

EPHESIANS 2:8–9

Pauline Epistles

Ephesians

WHAT IS EPHESIANS?

In this letter to the church at Ephesus, Paul calls the Ephesian believers to unity in Jesus because of the gift of salvation they have received. He writes that this unity is only possible through the power of the Holy Spirit.

EPHESIANS 2:1–10
FROM DEATH TO LIFE

[1] And you were dead in your trespasses and sins [2] in which you previously walked according to the ways of this world, according to the ruler of the power of the air, the spirit now working in the disobedient. [3] We too all previously lived among them in our fleshly desires, carrying out the inclinations of our flesh and thoughts, and we were by nature children under wrath as the others were also. [4] But God, who is rich in mercy, because of his great love that he had for us, [5] made us alive with Christ even though we were dead in trespasses. You are saved by grace! [6] He also raised us up with him and seated us with him in the heavens in Christ Jesus, [7] so that in the coming ages he might display the immeasurable riches of his grace through his kindness to us in Christ Jesus.

KEY VERSE

[8] For you are saved by grace through faith, and this is not from yourselves; it is God's gift— [9] not from works, so that no one can boast.

[10] For we are his workmanship, created in Christ Jesus for good works, which God prepared ahead of time for us to do.

EPHESIANS 4:1–6
UNITY AND DIVERSITY IN THE BODY OF CHRIST

[1] Therefore I, the prisoner in the Lord, urge you to walk worthy of the calling you have received, [2] with all humility and gentleness, with patience, bearing with one another in love, [3] making every effort to keep the unity of the Spirit through the bond of peace. [4] There is one body and one Spirit—just as you were called to one hope, at your calling—[5] one Lord, one faith, one baptism, [6] one God and Father of all, who is above all and through all and in all.

GENESIS 6:5–7
JUDGMENT DECREED

[5] When the LORD saw that human wickedness was widespread on the earth and that every inclination of the human mind was nothing but evil all the time, [6] the LORD regretted that he had made man on the earth, and he was deeply grieved. [7] Then the LORD said, "I will wipe mankind, whom I created, off the face of the earth, together with the animals, creatures that crawl, and birds of the sky—for I regret that I made them."

LAMENTATIONS 3:22–24

[22] Because of the LORD's faithful love
we do not perish,
for his mercies never end.
[23] They are new every morning;
great is your faithfulness!
[24] I say, "The LORD is my portion,
therefore I will put my hope in him."

JOHN 4:1–15
JESUS AND THE SAMARITAN WOMAN

[1] When Jesus learned that the Pharisees had heard he was making and baptizing more disciples than John [2] (though Jesus himself was not baptizing, but his disciples were), [3] he left Judea and went again to Galilee. [4] He had to travel through Samaria; [5] so he came to a town of Samaria called Sychar near the property that Jacob had given his son Joseph. [6] Jacob's well was there, and Jesus, worn out from his journey, sat down at the well. It was about noon.

[7] A woman of Samaria came to draw water.

"Give me a drink," Jesus said to her, [8] because his disciples had gone into town to buy food.

[9] "How is it that you, a Jew, ask for a drink from me, a Samaritan woman?" she asked him. For Jews do not associate with Samaritans.

[10] Jesus answered, "If you knew the gift of God, and who is saying to you, 'Give me a drink,' you would ask him, and he would give you living water."

[11] "Sir," said the woman, "you don't even have a bucket, and the well is deep. So where do you get this 'living water'? [12] You aren't greater than our father Jacob, are you? He gave us the well and drank from it himself, as did his sons and livestock."

[13] Jesus said, "Everyone who drinks from this water will get thirsty again. [14] But whoever drinks from the water that I will give him will never get thirsty again. In fact, the water I will give him will become a well of water springing up in him for eternal life."

[15] "Sir," the woman said to him, "give me this water so that I won't get thirsty and come here to draw water."

ROMANS 5:12–17
DEATH THROUGH ADAM AND LIFE THROUGH CHRIST

[12] Therefore, just as sin entered the world through one man, and death through sin, in this way death spread to all people, because all sinned. [13] In fact, sin was in the world before the law, but sin is not charged to a person's account when there is no law. [14] Nevertheless, death reigned from Adam to Moses, even over those who did not sin in the likeness of Adam's transgression. He is a type of the Coming One.

[15] But the gift is not like the trespass. For if by the one man's trespass the many died, how much more have the grace of God and the gift which comes through the grace of the one man Jesus Christ overflowed to the many. [16] And the gift is not like the one man's sin, because from one sin came the judgment, resulting in condemnation, but from many trespasses came the gift, resulting in justification. [17] If by the one man's trespass, death reigned through that one man, how much more will those who receive the overflow of grace and the gift of righteousness reign in life through the one man, Jesus Christ.

Key Verse

For you are saved by grace through faith, and this is not from yourselves; it is God's gift—not from works, so that no one can boast.

EPHESIANS 2:8–9

HOW EPHESIANS FITS IN THE STORY

Paul's letter to the Ephesians is an anthem to the grace of God displayed toward sinners in Christ. It contains some of the worst and best news in all of Scripture: we were once spiritually dead because of sin, but God made us alive through Christ. Because of this grace and the gift of salvation, we are called to live righteous lives.

COPY EPHESIANS 2:8–9 INTO THE SPACE PROVIDED ON PAGE 187.

1   Read Ephesians 2:1–6 again. According to verses 1–3, what were the conditions of our old life? According to verses 4–6, what are the conditions of our new life?

2   How does today's reading shape your understanding of the story of redemption?

RESPONSE

Triple Berry Salad with Candied Pecans

Ingredients

DRESSING

1 lemon, juice and zest

¼ teaspoon onion powder

½ teaspoon coarse ground Dijon mustard

¼ teaspoon salt

3 tablespoons white sugar

⅓ cup vegetable oil

½ tablespoon poppy seeds

SALAD

1 cup strawberries, rough chopped

1 cup raspberries, rough chopped

1 cup blackberries, rough chopped

8 ounces spinach and arugula mix

1 cup candied pecans

8 ounces goat cheese

Instructions

To make the dressing, blend all ingredients except for vegetable oil and poppy seeds in a food processor until completely smooth. Slowly pour in vegetable oil and blend. Stir in poppyseeds. (Dressing can be stored in the fridge in an airtight container for 4–5 days.)

Toss fruit with fresh greens, then sprinkle with pecans and cheese.

Drizzle the dressing on top right before serving, or serve on the side.

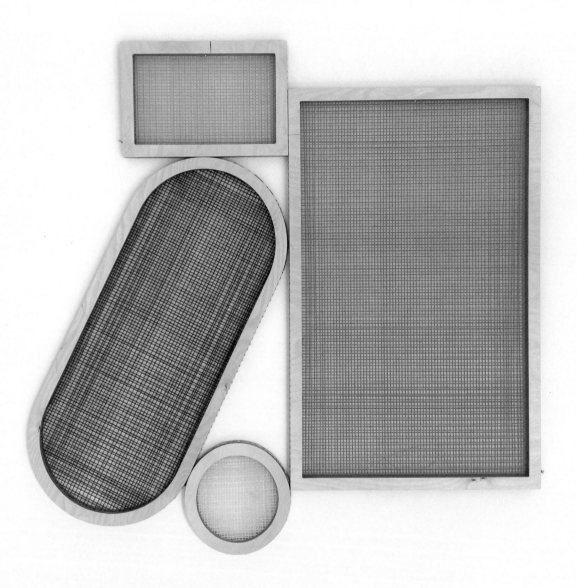

THIS IS THE NEW TESTAMENT

DAY 13

GRACE DAY

Take this day to catch up on your reading,
pray, and rest in the presence of the Lord.

Abram believed the LORD, and he credited it to him as righteousness.

GENESIS 15:6

DAY 14

WEEKLY TRUTH

Scripture is God-breathed and true. When we memorize it, we carry the good news of Jesus with us wherever we go.

As we survey the New Testament, we're memorizing Acts 13:27–31. This week, we'll work on adding verse 28. Each day, revisit this verse and say it aloud at least two times. See if you can recite both verses 27 and 28 from memory by the end of the week.

Though they found no grounds for the death sentence, they asked Pilate to have him killed.

ACTS 13:28

NOTES

Pauline Epistles

Philippians

WHAT IS PHILIPPIANS?

Philippians is one of Paul's warmest letters, written to thank the church in Philippi for a gift and to inform them of his imprisonment. This letter communicates that because of the eternal hope of the gospel, joy is possible in every circumstance.

PHILIPPIANS 1:12-30
ADVANCE OF THE GOSPEL

[12] Now I want you to know, brothers and sisters, that what has happened to me has actually advanced the gospel, [13] so that it has become known throughout the whole imperial guard, and to everyone else, that my imprisonment is because I am in Christ. [14] Most of the brothers have gained confidence in the Lord from my imprisonment and dare even more to speak the word fearlessly. [15] To be sure, some preach Christ out of envy and rivalry, but others out of good will. [16] These preach out of love, knowing that I am appointed for the defense of the gospel; [17] the others proclaim Christ out of selfish ambition, not sincerely, thinking that they will cause me trouble in my imprisonment. [18] What does it matter? Only that in every way, whether from false motives or true, Christ is proclaimed, and in this I rejoice. Yes, and I will continue to rejoice [19] because I know this will lead to my salvation through your prayers and help from the Spirit of

Jesus Christ. [20] My eager expectation and hope is that I will not be ashamed about anything, but that now as always, with all courage, Christ will be highly honored in my body, whether by life or by death.

LIVING IS CHRIST

[21] For me, to live is Christ and to die is gain.

[22] Now if I live on in the flesh, this means fruitful work for me; and I don't know which one I should choose. [23] I am torn between the two. I long to depart and be with Christ—which is far better— [24] but to remain in the flesh is more necessary for your sake. [25] Since I am persuaded of this, I know that I will remain and continue with all of you for your progress and joy in the faith, [26] so that, because of my coming to you again, your boasting in Christ Jesus may abound.

[27] Just one thing: As citizens of heaven, live your life worthy of the gospel of Christ. Then, whether I come and see you or am absent, I will hear about you that you are standing firm in one spirit, in one accord, contending together for the faith of the gospel, [28] not being frightened in any way by your opponents. This is a sign of destruction for them, but of your salvation—and this is from God. [29] For it has been granted to you on Christ's behalf not only to believe in him, but also to suffer for him, [30] since you are engaged in the same struggle that you saw I had and now hear that I have.

PHILIPPIANS 3:7-11

[7] But everything that was a gain to me, I have considered to be a loss because of Christ. [8] More than that, I also consider everything to be a loss in view of the surpassing value of knowing Christ Jesus my Lord. Because of him I have suffered the loss of all things and consider them as dung, so that I may gain Christ [9] and be found in him, not having a righteousness of my own from the law, but one that is through faith in Christ—the righteousness from God based on faith. [10] My goal is to know him and the power of his resurrection and the fellowship of his sufferings, being conformed to his death, [11] assuming that I will somehow reach the resurrection from among the dead.

ECCLESIASTES 3:1-15
THE MYSTERY OF TIME

[1] There is an occasion for everything,
and a time for every activity under heaven:
[2] a time to give birth and a time to die;
a time to plant and a time to uproot;
[3] a time to kill and a time to heal;
a time to tear down and a time to build;

[4] a time to weep and a time to laugh;
a time to mourn and a time to dance;
[5] a time to throw stones and a time to gather stones;
a time to embrace and a time to avoid embracing;
[6] a time to search and a time to count as lost;
a time to keep and a time to throw away;
[7] a time to tear and a time to sew;
a time to be silent and a time to speak;
[8] a time to love and a time to hate;
a time for war and a time for peace.

[9] What does the worker gain from his struggles? [10] I have seen the task that God has given the children of Adam to keep them occupied. [11] He has made everything appropriate in its time. He has also put eternity in their hearts, but no one can discover the work God has done from beginning to end. [12] I know that there is nothing better for them than to rejoice and enjoy the good life. [13] It is also the gift of God whenever anyone eats, drinks, and enjoys all his efforts. [14] I know that everything God does will last forever; there is no adding to it or taking from it. God works so that people will be in awe of him. [15] Whatever is, has already been, and whatever will be, already is. However, God seeks justice for the persecuted.

ROMANS 8:35–39

[35] Who can separate us from the love of Christ? Can affliction or distress or persecution or famine or nakedness or danger or sword? [36] As it is written:

Because of you
we are being put to death all day long;
we are counted as sheep to be slaughtered.

[37] No, in all these things we are more than conquerors through him who loved us. [38] For I am persuaded that neither death nor life, nor angels nor rulers, nor things present nor things to come, nor powers, [39] nor height nor depth, nor any other created thing will be able to separate us from the love of God that is in Christ Jesus our Lord.

Key Verse

For me, to live is Christ and to die is gain.

PHILIPPIANS 1:21

HOW PHILIPPIANS FITS IN THE STORY

Paul's letter to the Philippians teaches us about genuine Christian living. While nearly every theme he introduced here can also be found elsewhere in Scripture, this letter reveals how those themes impact our lives as believers. Philippians also contributes to our understanding of Christian commitment and what it means to be Christlike, even amidst suffering.

COPY PHILIPPIANS 1:21 INTO THE SPACE PROVIDED ON PAGE 187.

1 What do you long for in this world more than Jesus? How does Jesus ultimately satisfy that desire?

2 How does today's reading shape your understanding of the story of redemption?

RESPONSE

Colossians

WHAT IS COLOSSIANS?

Colossians is a letter written by Paul to counter false teaching in the city of Colossae. In it, Paul encourages Jewish and Gentile believers alike toward a proper understanding of the gospel of Jesus Christ. He also discusses the practical implications of salvation: because they have been made new in Jesus, their lives as believers should look different from their old lives.

COLOSSIANS 1:9–23
PRAYER FOR SPIRITUAL GROWTH

⁹ For this reason also, since the day we heard this, we haven't stopped praying for you. We are asking that you may be filled with the knowledge of his will in all wisdom and spiritual understanding, ¹⁰ so that you may walk worthy of the Lord, fully pleasing to him: bearing fruit in every good work and growing in the knowledge of God, ¹¹ being strengthened with all power, according to his glorious might, so that you may have great endurance and patience, joyfully ¹² giving thanks to the Father, who has enabled you to share in the saints' inheritance in the light. ¹³ He has rescued us from the domain of darkness and transferred us into the kingdom of the Son he loves. ¹⁴ In him we have redemption, the forgiveness of sins.

THE CENTRALITY OF CHRIST

¹⁵ He is the image of the invisible God,
the firstborn over all creation.
¹⁶ For everything was created by him,
in heaven and on earth,

the visible and the invisible,
whether thrones or dominions
or rulers or authorities—
all things have been created through him and for him.

KEY VERSE

¹⁷ He is before all things,
and by him all things hold together.

¹⁸ He is also the head of the body, the church;
he is the beginning,
the firstborn from the dead,
so that he might come to have
first place in everything.
¹⁹ For God was pleased to have
all his fullness dwell in him,
²⁰ and through him to reconcile
everything to himself,
whether things on earth or things in heaven,
by making peace
through his blood, shed on the cross.

²¹ Once you were alienated and hostile in your minds as expressed in your evil actions. ²² But now he has reconciled you by his physical body through his death, to present you holy, faultless, and blameless before him— ²³ if indeed you remain grounded and steadfast in the faith and are not shifted away from the hope of the gospel that you heard. This gospel has been proclaimed in all creation under heaven, and I, Paul, have become a servant of it.

COLOSSIANS 3:1-11

¹ So if you have been raised with Christ, seek the things above, where Christ is, seated at the right hand of God. ² Set your minds on things above, not on earthly things. ³ For you died, and your life is hidden with Christ in God. ⁴ When Christ, who is your life, appears, then you also will appear with him in glory.

⁵ Therefore, put to death what belongs to your earthly nature: sexual immorality, impurity, lust, evil desire, and greed, which is idolatry. ⁶ Because of these, God's wrath is coming upon the disobedient, ⁷ and you once walked in these things when you were living in them. ⁸ But now, put away all the following: anger, wrath, malice, slander, and filthy language from your mouth. ⁹ Do not lie to one another, since you have put off the old self with its practices ¹⁰ and have put on the new self. You are being renewed in knowledge according to the image of your Creator. ¹¹ In Christ there is not Greek and Jew, circumcision and uncircumcision, barbarian, Scythian, slave and free; but Christ is all and in all.

DANIEL 7:9–14

THE ANCIENT OF DAYS AND THE SON OF MAN

[9] As I kept watching,

thrones were set in place,
and the Ancient of Days took his seat.
His clothing was white like snow,
and the hair of his head like whitest wool.
His throne was flaming fire;
its wheels were blazing fire.
[10] A river of fire was flowing,
coming out from his presence.
Thousands upon thousands served him;
ten thousand times ten thousand stood before him.
The court was convened,
and the books were opened.

[11] I watched, then, because of the sound of the arrogant words the horn was speaking. As I continued watching, the beast was killed and its body destroyed and given over to the burning fire. [12] As for the rest of the beasts, their dominion was removed, but an extension of life was granted to them for a certain period of time. [13] I continued watching in the night visions,

and suddenly one like a son of man
was coming with the clouds of heaven.
He approached the Ancient of Days
and was escorted before him.
[14] He was given dominion
and glory and a kingdom,
so that those of every people,
nation, and language
should serve him.
His dominion is an everlasting dominion
that will not pass away,
and his kingdom is one
that will not be destroyed.

THE NATURE OF THE SON

[1] Long ago God spoke to our ancestors by the prophets at different times and in different ways. [2] In these last days, he has spoken to us by his Son. God has appointed him heir of all things and made the universe through him. [3] The Son is the radiance of God's glory and the exact expression of his nature, sustaining all things by his powerful word. After making purification for sins, he sat down at the right hand of the Majesty on high. [4] So he became superior to the angels, just as the name he inherited is more excellent than theirs.

DAY 16: COLOSSIANS

Key Verse

He is before all things, and by him all things hold together.

COLOSSIANS 1:17

HOW COLOSSIANS FITS IN THE STORY

Colossians provides one of the Bible's fullest expressions of Jesus's divine identity. This is most evident in the hymn of praise in Colossians 1:15–23, which presents Jesus as the image of the invisible God, the Creator and sustainer of the universe. He is the head of His body, the Church, and the One through whom forgiveness is possible.

COPY COLOSSIANS 1:17 INTO THE SPACE PROVIDED ON PAGE 187.

1 Jesus is both fully God and fully man. How does the hymn of praise in Colossians 1:15–23 encourage you to celebrate this truth?

2 How does today's reading shape your understanding of the story of redemption?

RESPONSE

Pauline Epistles

1 Thessalonians

WHAT IS 1 THESSALONIANS?

The book of 1 Thessalonians is Paul's letter of encouragement to the church in Thessalonica concerning their sustained faith in the midst of suffering. The letter served to correct misunderstandings about end-time events and to remind readers that continued sanctification is God's will for them.

1 THESSALONIANS 5:1–28
THE DAY OF THE LORD

[1] About the times and the seasons: Brothers and sisters, you do not need anything to be written to you. [2] For you yourselves know very well that the day of the Lord will come just like a thief in the night. [3] When they say, "Peace and security," then sudden destruction will come upon them, like labor pains on a pregnant woman, and they will not escape. [4] But you, brothers and sisters, are not in the dark, for this day to surprise you like a thief. [5] For you are all children of light and children of the day. We do not belong to the night or the darkness. [6] So then, let us not sleep, like the rest, but let us stay awake and be self-controlled. [7] For those who sleep, sleep at night, and those who get drunk, get drunk at night. [8] But since we belong to the day, let us be self-controlled and put on the armor of faith and love, and a helmet of the hope of salvation. [9] For God did not appoint us to wrath, but to obtain salvation through our Lord Jesus Christ, [10] who died for us, so that whether we are awake or asleep, we may live together with him. [11] Therefore encourage one another and build each other up as you are already doing.

¹² Now we ask you, brothers and sisters, to give recognition to those who labor among you and lead you in the Lord and admonish you, ¹³ and to regard them very highly in love because of their work. Be at peace among yourselves. ¹⁴ And we exhort you, brothers and sisters: warn those who are idle, comfort the discouraged, help the weak, be patient with everyone. ¹⁵ See to it that no one repays evil for evil to anyone, but always pursue what is good for one another and for all.

¹⁶ **Rejoice always,** ¹⁷ **pray constantly,** ¹⁸ **give thanks in everything; for this is God's will for you in Christ Jesus.**

KEY VERSE

¹⁹ Don't stifle the Spirit. ²⁰ Don't despise prophecies, ²¹ but test all things. Hold on to what is good. ²² Stay away from every kind of evil.

²³ Now may the God of peace himself sanctify you completely. And may your whole spirit, soul, and body be kept sound and blameless at the coming of our Lord Jesus Christ. ²⁴ He who calls you is faithful; he will do it. ²⁵ Brothers and sisters, pray for us also. ²⁶ Greet all the brothers and sisters with a holy kiss. ²⁷ I charge you by the Lord that this letter be read to all the brothers and sisters. ²⁸ The grace of our Lord Jesus Christ be with you.

DEUTERONOMY 6:4–9

⁴ Listen, Israel: The LORD our God, the LORD is one. ⁵ Love the LORD your God with all your heart, with all your soul, and with all your strength. ⁶ These words that I am giving you today are to be in your heart. ⁷ Repeat them to your children. Talk about them when you sit in your house and when you walk along the road, when you lie down and when you get up. ⁸ Bind them as a sign on your hand and let them be a symbol on your forehead. ⁹ Write them on the doorposts of your house and on your city gates.

MATTHEW 11:28–30

²⁸ "Come to me, all of you who are weary and burdened, and I will give you rest. ²⁹ Take up my yoke and learn from me, because I am lowly and humble in heart, and you will find rest for your souls. ³⁰ For my yoke is easy and my burden is light."

ROMANS 12:1–2
A LIVING SACRIFICE

¹ Therefore, brothers and sisters, in view of the mercies of God, I urge you to present your bodies as a living sacrifice, holy and pleasing to God; this is your true worship. ² Do not be conformed to this age, but be transformed by the renewing of your mind, so that you may discern what is the good, pleasing, and perfect will of God.

JAMES 3:13–18
THE WISDOM FROM ABOVE

¹³ Who among you is wise and understanding? By his good conduct he should show that his works are done in the gentleness that comes from wisdom. ¹⁴ But if you have bitter envy and selfish ambition in your heart, don't boast and deny the truth. ¹⁵ Such wisdom does not come down from above but is earthly, unspiritual, demonic. ¹⁶ For where there is envy and selfish ambition, there is disorder and every evil practice. ¹⁷ But the wisdom from above is first pure, then peace-loving, gentle, compliant, full of mercy and good fruits, unwavering, without pretense. ¹⁸ And the fruit of righteousness is sown in peace by those who cultivate peace.

Key Verse

Rejoice always, pray constantly, give thanks in everything; for this is God's will for you in Christ Jesus.

1 THESSALONIANS 5:16–18

HOW 1 THESSALONIANS FITS IN THE STORY

First Thessalonians contributes to our understanding of the second coming of Christ. Paul wrote this letter to correct the church's misunderstandings of this teaching and, in the process, show that Christ's eventual return gives us true hope in all circumstances. He also speaks to the practices that make us more like Christ.

COPY 1 THESSALONIANS 5:16–18 INTO THE SPACE PROVIDED ON PAGE 187.

1 How can the acts of rejoicing, prayer, and thanksgiving train and develop believers to become more like Christ? How does this mindset provide comfort in every season?

2 How does today's reading shape your understanding of the story of redemption?

A TIMELINE OF THE NEW TESTAMENT

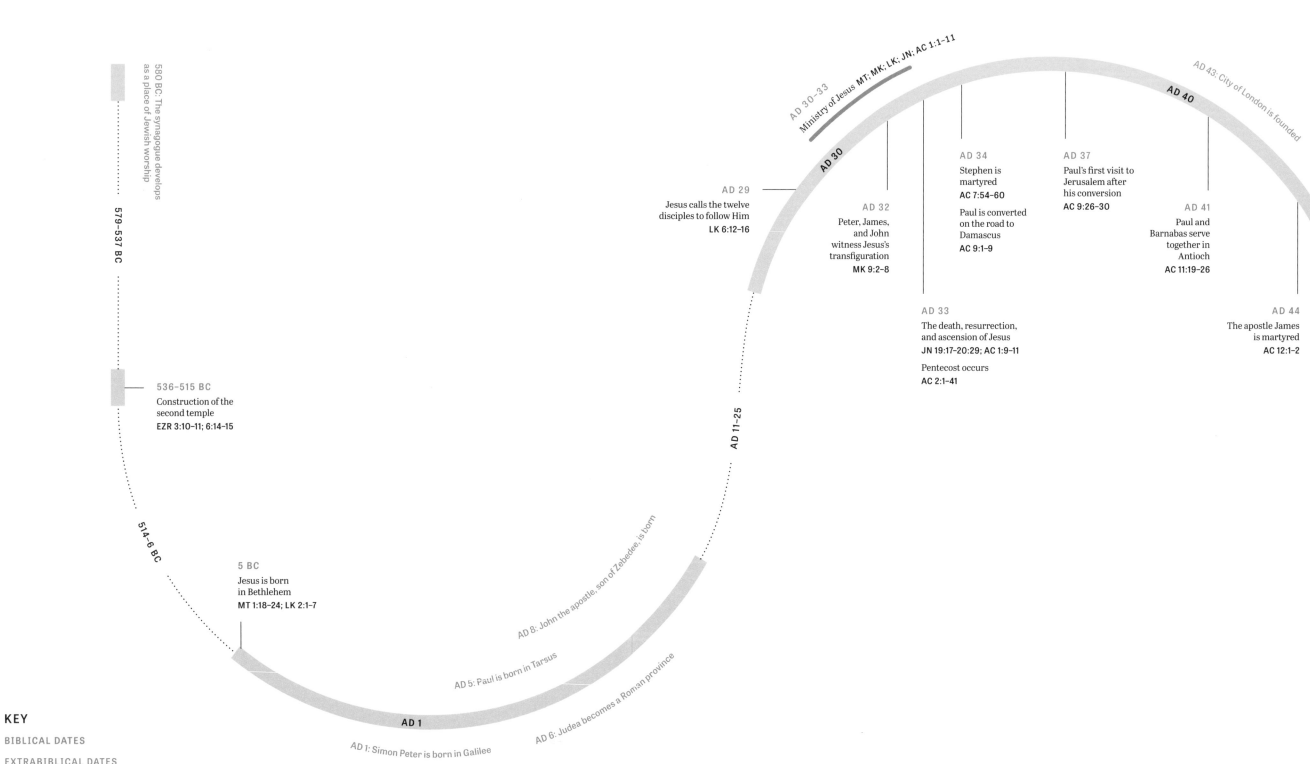

580 BC: The synagogue develops as a place of Jewish worship

579–537 BC

536–515 BC
Construction of the second temple
EZR 3:10–11; 6:14–15

514–6 BC

5 BC
Jesus is born in Bethlehem
MT 1:18–24; LK 2:1–7

AD 1: Simon Peter is born in Galilee

AD 1

AD 5: Paul is born in Tarsus

AD 6: Judea becomes a Roman province

AD 8: John the apostle, son of Zebedee, is born

AD 11–25

AD 29
Jesus calls the twelve disciples to follow Him
LK 6:12–16

AD 30–33
Ministry of Jesus MT; MK; LK; JN; AC 1:1–11

AD 30

AD 32
Peter, James, and John witness Jesus's transfiguration
MK 9:2–8

AD 33
The death, resurrection, and ascension of Jesus
JN 19:17–20:29; AC 1:9–11

Pentecost occurs
AC 2:1–41

AD 34
Stephen is martyred
AC 7:54–60

Paul is converted on the road to Damascus
AC 9:1–9

AD 37
Paul's first visit to Jerusalem after his conversion
AC 9:26–30

AD 40

AD 41
Paul and Barnabas serve together in Antioch
AC 11:19–26

AD 43: City of London is founded

AD 44
The apostle James is martyred
AC 12:1–2

KEY

BIBLICAL DATES

EXTRABIBLICAL DATES

BOOKS OF THE NEW TESTAMENT

Though the dates in this timeline have been carefully researched, scholars disagree on the precise year of Jesus's birth and the duration of His ministry prior to His crucifixion.

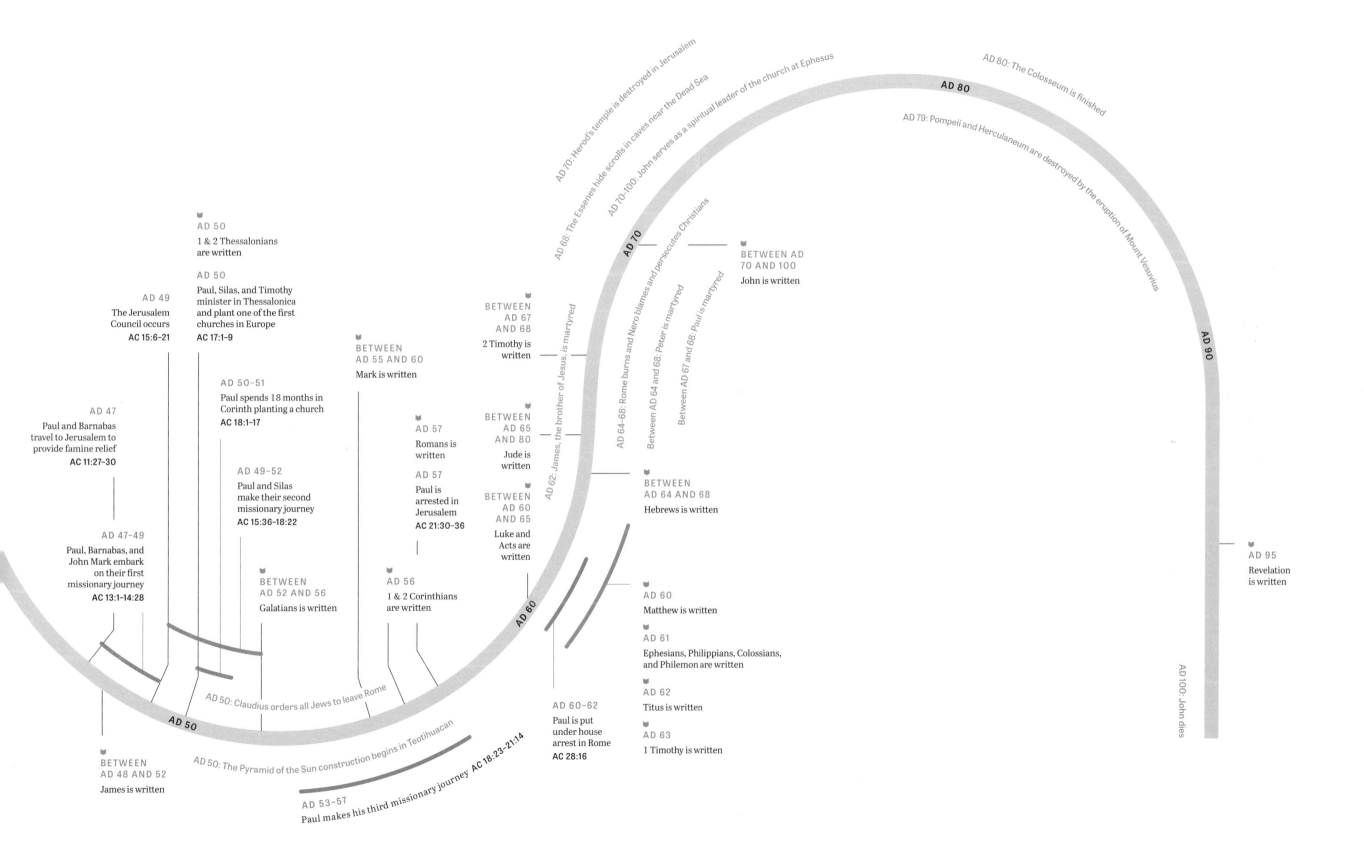

AD 70: Herod's temple is destroyed in Jerusalem

AD 68: The Essenes hide scrolls in caves near the Dead Sea

AD 70–100: John serves as a spiritual leader of the church at Ephesus

AD 80: The Colosseum is finished

AD 80

AD 79: Pompeii and Herculaneum are destroyed by the eruption of Mount Vesuvius

AD 70

AD 90

AD 50

1 & 2 Thessalonians
are written

AD 50

Paul, Silas, and Timothy
minister in Thessalonica
and plant one of the first
churches in Europe
AC 17:1–9

AD 49

The Jerusalem
Council occurs
AC 15:6–21

BETWEEN
AD 67
AND 68

2 Timothy is
written

AD 64–68: Rome burns and Nero blames and persecutes Christians

Between AD 64 and 68: Peter is martyred

Between AD 67 and 68: Paul is martyred

BETWEEN AD
70 AND 100

John is written

AD 50–51

Paul spends 18 months in
Corinth planting a church
AC 18:1–17

BETWEEN
AD 55 AND 60

Mark is written

AD 47

Paul and Barnabas
travel to Jerusalem to
provide famine relief
AC 11:27–30

AD 57

Romans is
written

BETWEEN
AD 65
AND 80

Jude is
written

AD 62: James, the brother of Jesus, is martyred

AD 49–52

Paul and Silas
make their second
missionary journey
AC 15:36–18:22

AD 57

Paul is
arrested in
Jerusalem
AC 21:30–36

BETWEEN
AD 60
AND 65

Luke and
Acts are
written

BETWEEN
AD 64 AND 68

Hebrews is written

AD 95

Revelation
is written

AD 47–49

Paul, Barnabas, and
John Mark embark
on their first
missionary journey
AC 13:1–14:28

BETWEEN
AD 52 AND 56

Galatians is written

AD 56

1 & 2 Corinthians
are written

AD 60

Matthew is written

AD 61

Ephesians, Philippians, Colossians,
and Philemon are written

AD 50: Claudius orders all Jews to leave Rome

AD 60

AD 62

Titus is written

AD 50

AD 60–62

Paul is put
under house
arrest in Rome
AC 28:16

AD 63

1 Timothy is written

AD 100: John dies

AD 50: The Pyramid of the Sun construction begins in Teotihuacan

BETWEEN
AD 48 AND 52

James is written

AD 53–57

Paul makes his third missionary journey AC 18:23–21:14

The following timeline contains the approximate date of key events throughout the New Testament, along with historical events from outside the biblical narrative, to aid you in your study of the greater narrative of Scripture. You will find Scripture references below biblical events so you can explore these stories in their context.

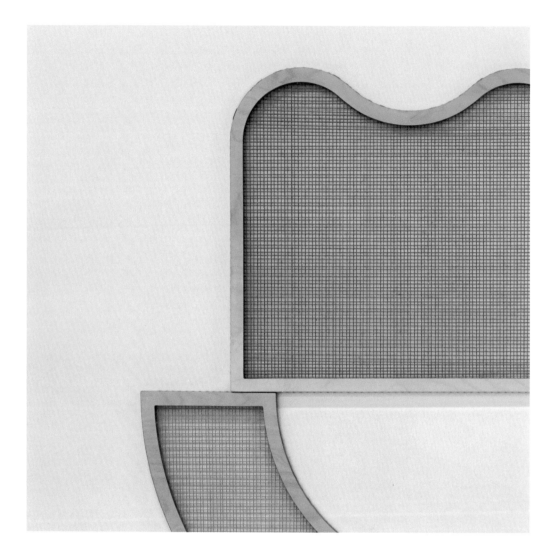

May the Lord direct your hearts to God's love and Christ's endurance.

2 THESSALONIANS 3:5

Pauline Epistles

2 Thessalonians

WHAT IS 2 THESSALONIANS?

A follow-up to Paul's first letter to the church in Thessalonica, the book of 2 Thessalonians offers further clarification on how to live the Christian life in light of Christ's promised return. This letter calls believers to stand firm in their faith, following Christ's example.

2 THESSALONIANS 2:13–17
STAND FIRM

[13] But we ought to thank God always for you, brothers and sisters loved by the Lord, because from the beginning God has chosen you for salvation through sanctification by the Spirit and through belief in the truth. [14] He called you to this through our gospel, so that you might obtain the glory of our Lord Jesus Christ. [15] So then, brothers and sisters, stand firm and hold to the traditions you were taught, whether by what we said or what we wrote.

[16] May our Lord Jesus Christ himself and God our Father, who has loved us and given us eternal encouragement and good hope by grace, [17] encourage your hearts and strengthen you in every good work and word.

2 THESSALONIANS 3:1–5
PRAY FOR US

[1] In addition, brothers and sisters, pray for us that the word of the Lord may spread rapidly and be honored, just as it was

with you, ² and that we may be delivered from wicked and evil people, for not all have faith. ³ But the Lord is faithful; he will strengthen you and guard you from the evil one. ⁴ We have confidence in the Lord about you, that you are doing and will continue to do what we command.

KEY VERSE

⁵ May the Lord direct your hearts to God's love and Christ's endurance.

PSALM 22:25–31

²⁵ I will give praise in the great assembly
because of you;
I will fulfill my vows
before those who fear you.
²⁶ The humble will eat and be satisfied;
those who seek the LORD will praise him.
May your hearts live forever!

²⁷ All the ends of the earth will remember
and turn to the LORD.
All the families of the nations
will bow down before you,
²⁸ for kingship belongs to the LORD;
he rules the nations.
²⁹ All who prosper on earth will eat and bow down;
all those who go down to the dust
will kneel before him—
even the one who cannot preserve his life.
³⁰ Their descendants will serve him;
the next generation will be told about the Lord.
³¹ They will come and declare his righteousness;
to a people yet to be born
they will declare what he has done.

MATTHEW 26:36–46
THE PRAYER IN THE GARDEN

³⁶ Then Jesus came with them to a place called Gethsemane, and he told the disciples, "Sit here while I go over there and pray." ³⁷ Taking along Peter and the two sons of Zebedee, he began to be sorrowful and troubled. ³⁸ He said to them, "I am deeply grieved to the point of death. Remain here and stay awake with me." ³⁹ Going a little farther, he fell facedown and prayed, "My Father, if it is possible, let this cup pass from me. Yet not as I will, but as you will."

⁴⁰ Then he came to the disciples and found them sleeping. He asked Peter, "So, couldn't you stay awake with me one hour? ⁴¹ Stay awake and pray, so that you won't enter into temptation. The spirit is willing, but the flesh is weak."

⁴² Again, a second time, he went away and prayed, "My Father, if this cannot pass unless I drink it, your will be done." ⁴³ And he came again and found them sleeping, because they could not keep their eyes open.

⁴⁴ After leaving them, he went away again and prayed a third time, saying the same thing once more. ⁴⁵ Then he came to the disciples and said to them, "Are you still sleeping and resting? See, the time is near. The Son of Man is betrayed into the hands of sinners. ⁴⁶ Get up; let's go. See, my betrayer is near."

HEBREWS 12:1–2
THE CALL TO ENDURANCE

¹ Therefore, since we also have such a large cloud of witnesses surrounding us, let us lay aside every hindrance and the sin that so easily ensnares us. Let us run with endurance the race that lies before us, ² keeping our eyes on Jesus, the pioneer and perfecter of our faith. For the joy that lay before him, he endured the cross, despising the shame, and sat down at the right hand of the throne of God.

JAMES 5:7–11
WAITING FOR THE LORD

⁷ Therefore, brothers and sisters, be patient until the Lord's coming. See how the farmer waits for the precious fruit of the earth and is patient with it until it receives the early and the late rains. ⁸ You also must be patient. Strengthen your hearts, because the Lord's coming is near.

⁹ Brothers and sisters, do not complain about one another, so that you will not be judged. Look, the judge stands at the door!

¹⁰ Brothers and sisters, take the prophets who spoke in the Lord's name as an example of suffering and patience. ¹¹ See, we count as blessed those who have endured. You have heard of Job's endurance and have seen the outcome that the Lord brought about—the Lord is compassionate and merciful.

Key Verse

May the Lord direct your hearts to God's love and Christ's endurance.

2 THESSALONIANS 3:5

HOW 2 THESSALONIANS FITS IN THE STORY

Second Thessalonians continues the themes found in 1 Thessalonians: persecution, sanctification, and the second coming of Jesus. The letter proclaims that salvation in Christ, though already secured, will be ultimately fulfilled when He comes again, overthrowing evil and bringing rest and glory. This letter reminds us that God loves His people and gives them great comfort and hope, even in the midst of persecution.

COPY 2 THESSALONIANS 3:5 INTO THE SPACE PROVIDED ON PAGE 187.

1　　How does Christ's endurance provide you with hope in your current circumstances?

2　　How does today's reading shape your understanding of the story of redemption?

RESPONSE

This saying is trustworthy and deserving of full acceptance: "Christ Jesus came into the world to save sinners"—and I am the worst of them.

1 TIMOTHY 1:15

Pauline Epistles

1 Timothy

WHAT IS 1 TIMOTHY?

The book of 1 Timothy is Paul's letter to his co-laborer and son in the faith, Timothy. In it, he gives instructions for order and structure in the church and warns Timothy to replace false teaching with sound doctrine. Paul also offers practical advice on humble leadership for the young pastor and the church he leads.

1 TIMOTHY 1:12–17
PAUL'S TESTIMONY

¹² I give thanks to Christ Jesus our Lord who has strengthened me, because he considered me faithful, appointing me to the ministry— ¹³ even though I was formerly a blasphemer, a persecutor, and an arrogant man. But I received mercy because I acted out of ignorance in unbelief, ¹⁴ and the grace of our Lord overflowed, along with the faith and love that are in Christ Jesus.

KEY VERSE

¹⁵ This saying is trustworthy and deserving of full acceptance: "Christ Jesus came into the world to save sinners"—and I am the worst of them.

¹⁶ But I received mercy for this reason, so that in me, the worst of them, Christ Jesus might demonstrate his extraordinary patience as an example to those who would believe in him for eternal life. ¹⁷ Now to the King eternal, immortal, invisible, the only God, be honor and glory forever and ever. Amen.

1 TIMOTHY 4:7–10

[7] But have nothing to do with pointless and silly myths. Rather, train yourself in godliness. [8] For the training of the body has limited benefit, but godliness is beneficial in every way, since it holds promise for the present life and also for the life to come. [9] This saying is trustworthy and deserves full acceptance. [10] For this reason we labor and strive, because we have put our hope in the living God, who is the Savior of all people, especially of those who believe.

1 CHRONICLES 29:10–19

DAVID'S PRAYER

[10] Then David blessed the Lord in the sight of all the assembly. David said,

May you be blessed, Lord God of our father Israel, from eternity to eternity. [11] Yours, Lord, is the greatness and the power and the glory and the splendor and the majesty, for everything in the heavens and on earth belongs to you. Yours, Lord, is the kingdom, and you are exalted as head over all. [12] Riches and honor come from you, and you are the ruler of everything. Power and might are in your hand, and it is in your hand to make great and to give strength to all. [13] Now therefore, our God, we give you thanks and praise your glorious name.

[14] But who am I, and who are my people, that we should be able to give as generously as this? For everything comes from you, and we have given you only what comes from your own hand. [15] For we are aliens and temporary residents in your presence as were all our ancestors. Our days on earth are like a shadow, without hope. [16] Lord our God, all this wealth that we've provided for building you a house for your holy name comes from your hand; everything belongs to you. [17] I know, my God, that you test the heart and that you are pleased with what is right. I have willingly given all these things with an upright heart, and now I have seen your people who are present here giving joyfully and willingly to you. [18] Lord God of Abraham, Isaac, and Israel, our ancestors, keep this desire forever in the thoughts of the hearts of your people, and confirm their hearts toward you. [19] Give my son Solomon an undivided heart to keep and to carry out all your commands, your decrees, and your statutes, and to build the building for which I have made provision.

PROVERBS 28:13

The one who conceals his sins
will not prosper,
but whoever confesses and renounces them
will find mercy.

TEACHINGS ON HUMILITY

[7] He told a parable to those who were invited, when he noticed how they would choose the best places for themselves: [8] "When you are invited by someone to a wedding banquet, don't sit in the place of honor, because a more distinguished person than you may have been invited by your host. [9] The one who invited both of you may come and say to you, 'Give your place to this man,' and then in humiliation, you will proceed to take the lowest place.

[10] "But when you are invited, go and sit in the lowest place, so that when the one who invited you comes, he will say to you, 'Friend, move up higher.' You will then be honored in the presence of all the other guests. [11] For everyone who exalts himself will be humbled, and the one who humbles himself will be exalted."

1 PETER 5:5–7

[5] In the same way, you who are younger, be subject to the elders. All of you clothe yourselves with humility toward one another, because

God resists the proud
but gives grace to the humble.

[6] Humble yourselves, therefore, under the mighty hand of God, so that he may exalt you at the proper time, [7] casting all your cares on him, because he cares about you.

Key Verse

This saying is trustworthy and deserving of full acceptance: "Christ Jesus came into the world to save sinners"—and I am the worst of them.

1 TIMOTHY 1:15

HOW 1 TIMOTHY FITS IN THE STORY

First Timothy offers rich theological and ethical wisdom. Here, Paul draws a direct connection between belief and behavior. While 1 Timothy, 2 Timothy, and Titus were not intended to provide a detailed account of church government, they do provide significant insights on the topic, such as a list of characteristics for overseers and deacons. In describing the character and nature of a Christlike leader, the letter also gives a model for all believers.

COPY 1 TIMOTHY 1:15 INTO THE SPACE PROVIDED ON PAGE 188.

1   How does a humble disposition equip you for the ministry and work you have been called to?

2   How does today's reading shape your understanding of the story of redemption?

RESPONSE

Mini Pizza Popovers

Ingredients

1 17.5-ounce package frozen puff pastry, thawed

1 cup fresh basil

8 ounces deli pepperoni

4 ounces mozzarella cheese, shredded

1 egg, beaten, mixed with 1 tablespoon water

Instructions

Preheat the oven to 400°F. Line two large baking sheets with parchment paper.

Lay out a sheet of puff pastry on one of the prepared baking sheets and cut into four squares. Repeat on the other baking sheet so you have eight squares spread evenly across both trays.

Layer the basil leaves, pepperoni, and cheese on one half of each pastry square.

Fold over the uncovered sides of each pastry, brushing with the egg mixture to help edges stick together.

Bake until golden and puffy, about 15 minutes. Serve warm.

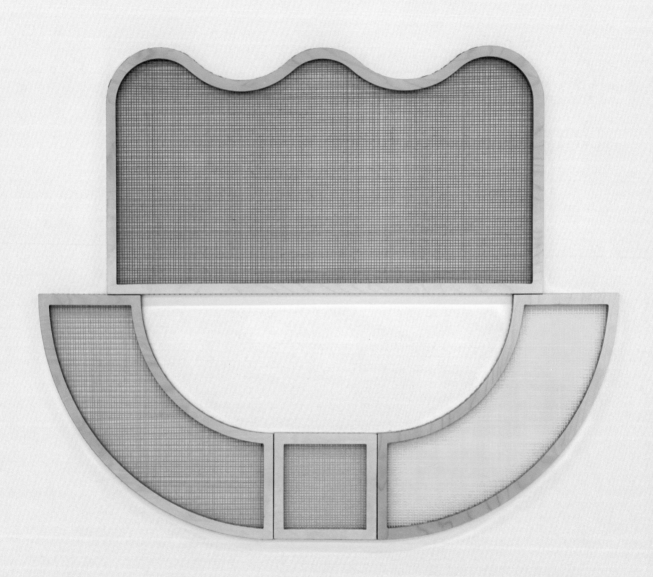

DAY 20

GRACE DAY

Take this day to catch up on your reading,
pray, and rest in the presence of the Lord.

He was given dominion and
glory and a kingdom, so that
those of every people, nation,
and language should serve him.
His dominion is an everlasting
dominion that will not pass
away, and his kingdom is one
that will not be destroyed.

DANIEL 7:14

WEEKLY TRUTH

Scripture is God-breathed and true. When we memorize it, we carry the good news of Jesus with us wherever we go.

This week we will continue memorizing Paul's sermon in Acts 13 by adding verse 29. Start by reciting what you've already memorized out loud. Then underline each verb in verse 29. As you work on memorizing this verse, try emphasizing the verbs as you repeat the verse aloud.

When they had carried out all that had been written about him, they took him down from the tree and put him in a tomb.

ACTS 13:29

NOTES

DAY 22

Pauline Epistles

2 Timothy

WHAT IS 2 TIMOTHY?

Second Timothy, also written to Paul's son in the faith Timothy, is the last letter Paul wrote before he was martyred in Rome. It encourages endurance for believers and stresses the importance of teaching God's Word to the believers entrusted to his care.

2 TIMOTHY 3:10–17
STRUGGLES IN THE CHRISTIAN LIFE

[10] But you have followed my teaching, conduct, purpose, faith, patience, love, and endurance, [11] along with the persecutions and sufferings that came to me in Antioch, Iconium, and Lystra. What persecutions I endured—and yet the Lord rescued me from them all. [12] In fact, all who want to live a godly life in Christ Jesus will be persecuted. [13] Evil people and impostors will become worse, deceiving and being deceived. [14] But as for you, continue in what you have learned and firmly believed. You know those who taught you, [15] and you know that from infancy you have known the sacred Scriptures, which are able to give you wisdom for salvation through faith in Christ Jesus.

KEY VERSE

[16] All Scripture is inspired by God and is profitable for teaching, for rebuking, for correcting, for training in righteousness, [17] so that the man of God may be complete, equipped for every good work.

2 TIMOTHY 4:1–8
FULFILL YOUR MINISTRY

[1] I solemnly charge you before God and Christ Jesus, who is going to judge the living and the dead, and because of his appearing and his kingdom: [2] Preach the word; be ready in season and out of season; correct, rebuke, and encourage with great patience and teaching. [3] For the time will come when people will not tolerate sound doctrine, but according to their own desires, will multiply teachers for themselves because they have an itch to hear what they want to hear. [4] They will turn away from hearing the truth and will turn aside to myths. [5] But as for you, exercise self-control in everything, endure hardship, do the work of an evangelist, fulfill your ministry.

[6] For I am already being poured out as a drink offering, and the time for my departure is close. [7] I have fought the good fight, I have finished the race, I have kept the faith. [8] There is reserved for me the crown of righteousness, which the Lord, the righteous Judge, will give me on that day, and not only to me, but to all those who have loved his appearing.

DEUTERONOMY 8:1–11
REMEMBER THE LORD

[1] Carefully follow every command I am giving you today, so that you may live and increase, and may enter and take possession of the land the LORD swore to your ancestors. [2] Remember that the LORD your God led you on the entire journey these forty years in the wilderness, so that he might humble you and test you to know what was in your heart, whether or not you would keep his commands. [3] He humbled you by letting you go hungry; then he gave you manna to eat, which you and your ancestors had not known, so that you might learn that man does not live on bread alone but on every word that comes from the mouth of the LORD. [4] Your clothing did not wear out, and your feet did not swell these forty years. [5] Keep in mind that the LORD your God has been disciplining you just as a man disciplines his son. [6] So keep the commands of the LORD your God by walking in his ways and fearing him. [7] For the LORD your God is bringing you into a good land, a land with streams, springs, and deep water sources, flowing in both valleys and hills; [8] a land of wheat, barley, vines, figs, and pomegranates; a land of olive oil and honey; [9] a land where you will eat food without shortage, where you will lack nothing; a land whose rocks are iron and from whose hills you will mine copper. [10] When you eat and are full, you will bless the LORD your God for the good land he has given you.

[11] Be careful that you don't forget the LORD your God by failing to keep his commands, ordinances, and statutes that I am giving you today.

JOSHUA 1:7–9

[7] "Above all, be strong and very courageous to observe carefully the whole instruction my servant Moses commanded you. Do not turn from it to the right or the left, so that you will have success wherever you go. [8] This book of instruction must not depart from your mouth; you are to meditate on it day and night so that you may carefully observe everything written in it. For then you will prosper and succeed in whatever you do. [9] Haven't I commanded you: be strong and courageous? Do not be afraid or discouraged, for the LORD your God is with you wherever you go."

PROVERBS 3:1–6
TRUST THE LORD

[1] My son, don't forget my teaching,
but let your heart keep my commands;
[2] for they will bring you
many days, a full life, and well-being.
[3] Never let loyalty and faithfulness leave you.
Tie them around your neck;
write them on the tablet of your heart.
[4] Then you will find favor and high regard
with God and people.

[5] Trust in the LORD with all your heart,
and do not rely on your own understanding;
[6] in all your ways know him,
and he will make your paths straight.

ROMANS 15:4–6

[4] For whatever was written in the past was written for our instruction, so that we may have hope through endurance and through the encouragement from the Scriptures. [5] Now may the God who gives endurance and encouragement grant you to live in harmony with one another, according to Christ Jesus, [6] so that you may glorify the God and Father of our Lord Jesus Christ with one mind and one voice.

Key Verse

All Scripture is inspired by God and is profitable for teaching, for rebuking, for correcting, for training in righteousness, so that the man of God may be complete, equipped for every good work.

2 TIMOTHY 3:16–17

HOW 2 TIMOTHY FITS IN THE STORY

As Paul built up church leaders, he expressed concern for spreading the truth of the gospel. His faithfulness in refuting false gospels laid a significant foundation for the early Church, as well as for believers today. Second Timothy gives insight into Paul's perspective of hope in suffering through extremely difficult circumstances.

COPY 2 TIMOTHY 3:16–17 INTO THE SPACE PROVIDED ON PAGE 188.

1   How does God's Word equip you for "every good work" (2Tim 3:17)?

2   How does today's reading shape your understanding of the story of redemption?

DAY 23

Pauline Epistles

Titus

WHAT IS TITUS?

The book of Titus is Paul's letter of encouragement to Titus, a pastor, beloved friend, and son in the faith. This letter covers similar themes to those found in 1 & 2 Timothy. It warns against false teachers and gives instruction for how Christians should live because of the grace shown to them in Christ.

TITUS 2:11-15

[11] For the grace of God has appeared, bringing salvation for all people, [12] instructing us to deny godlessness and worldly lusts and to live in a sensible, righteous, and godly way in the present age, [13] while we wait for the blessed hope, the appearing of the glory of our great God and Savior, Jesus Christ. [14] He gave himself for us to redeem us from all lawlessness and to cleanse for himself a people for his own possession, eager to do good works.

[15] Proclaim these things; encourage and rebuke with all authority. Let no one disregard you.

TITUS 3:1-7
CHRISTIAN LIVING AMONG OUTSIDERS

[1] Remind them to submit to rulers and authorities, to obey, to be ready for every good work, [2] to slander no one, to avoid fighting, and to be kind, always showing gentleness to all people. [3] For we too were once foolish, disobedient, deceived, enslaved by various passions and pleasures, living in malice and envy, hateful, detesting one another.

4 But when the kindness of God our Savior and his love for mankind appeared,

KEY VERSE

5 he saved us—not by works of righteousness that we had done, but according to his mercy—through the washing of regeneration and renewal by the Holy Spirit.

6 He poured out his Spirit on us abundantly through Jesus Christ our Savior 7 so that, having been justified by his grace, we may become heirs with the hope of eternal life.

MICAH 7:18-19

18 Who is a God like you,
forgiving iniquity and passing over rebellion
for the remnant of his inheritance?
He does not hold on to his anger forever
because he delights in faithful love.
19 He will again have compassion on us;
he will vanquish our iniquities.
You will cast all our sins
into the depths of the sea.

MATTHEW 5:13-16

BELIEVERS ARE SALT AND LIGHT

13 "You are the salt of the earth. But if the salt should lose its taste, how can it be made salty? It's no longer good for anything but to be thrown out and trampled under people's feet.

14 "You are the light of the world. A city situated on a hill cannot be hidden. 15 No one lights a lamp and puts it under a basket, but rather on a lampstand, and it gives light for all who are in the house. 16 In the same way, let your light shine before others, so that they may see your good works and give glory to your Father in heaven."

1 JOHN 3:1-3

1 See what great love the Father has given us that we should be called God's children—and we are! The reason the world does not know us is that it didn't know him. 2 Dear friends, we are God's children now, and what we will be has not yet been revealed. We know that when he appears, we will be like him because we will see him as he is. 3 And everyone who has this hope in him purifies himself just as he is pure.

Key Verse

He saved us—not by works of righteousness that we had done, but according to his mercy—through the washing of regeneration and renewal by the Holy Spirit.

TITUS 3:5

HOW TITUS FITS IN THE STORY

Paul fought for the spiritual health and maturity of Titus by making clear the connection between a follower of Christ's faith and their behavior. The book of Titus acknowledges that believers can be tempted to live in ways that contradict the faith they profess. Paul points to the salvation we have in Christ Jesus as motivation and foundation for living out this new way of life.

COPY TITUS 3:5 INTO THE SPACE PROVIDED ON PAGE 188.

1 How does today's reading from Titus about God's kindness toward you impact your relationship with Him?

2 How does today's reading shape your understanding of the story of redemption?

RESPONSE

Pauline Epistles

Philemon

WHAT IS PHILEMON?

Paul wrote this short letter to Philemon, a leader of the house church in Colossae, during his first imprisonment in Rome. In it, Paul asks his friend to forgive Onesimus, who was enslaved to Philemon and came to faith after running away and meeting Paul. Paul also asks Philemon to restore Onesimus to his household, demonstrating Christian love by treating him as a brother in Christ.

PHILEMON 4–22
PHILEMON'S LOVE AND FAITH

⁴ I always thank my God when I mention you in my prayers, ⁵ because I hear of your love for all the saints and the faith that you have in the Lord Jesus. ⁶ I pray that your participation in the faith may become effective through knowing every good thing that is in us for the glory of Christ. ⁷ For I have great joy and encouragement from your love, because the hearts of the saints have been refreshed through you, brother.

AN APPEAL FOR ONESIMUS

KEY VERSE

⁸ For this reason, although I have great boldness in Christ to command you to do what is right, ⁹ I appeal to you, instead, on the basis of love.

I, Paul, as an elderly man and now also as a prisoner of Christ Jesus, ¹⁰ appeal to you for my son, Onesimus. I became his father while I was in chains. ¹¹ Once he was useless to you,

but now he is useful both to you and to me. [12] I am sending him back to you—I am sending my very own heart. [13] I wanted to keep him with me, so that in my imprisonment for the gospel he might serve me in your place. [14] But I didn't want to do anything without your consent, so that your good deed might not be out of obligation, but of your own free will. [15] For perhaps this is why he was separated from you for a brief time, so that you might get him back permanently, [16] no longer as a slave, but more than a slave—as a dearly loved brother. He is especially so to me, but how much more to you, both in the flesh and in the Lord.

[17] So if you consider me a partner, welcome him as you would me. [18] And if he has wronged you in any way, or owes you anything, charge that to my account. [19] I, Paul, write this with my own hand: I will repay it—not to mention to you that you owe me even your very self. [20] Yes, brother, may I benefit from you in the Lord; refresh my heart in Christ. [21] Since I am confident of your obedience, I am writing to you, knowing that you will do even more than I say. [22] Meanwhile, also prepare a guest room for me, since I hope that through your prayers I will be restored to you.

LEVITICUS 19:11–18

[11] "Do not steal. Do not act deceptively or lie to one another. [12] Do not swear falsely by my name, profaning the name of your God; I am the LORD.

[13] "Do not oppress your neighbor or rob him. The wages due a hired worker must not remain with you until morning. [14] Do not curse the deaf or put a stumbling block in front of the blind, but you are to fear your God; I am the LORD.

[15] "Do not act unjustly when deciding a case. Do not be partial to the poor or give preference to the rich; judge your neighbor fairly. [16] Do not go about spreading slander among your people; do not jeopardize your neighbor's life; I am the LORD.

[17] "Do not harbor hatred against your brother. Rebuke your neighbor directly, and you will not incur guilt because of him. [18] Do not take revenge or bear a grudge against members of your community, but love your neighbor as yourself; I am the LORD."

1 CORINTHIANS 13
LOVE: THE SUPERIOR WAY

[1] If I speak human or angelic tongues but do not have love, I am a noisy gong or a clanging cymbal. [2] If I have the gift of prophecy and understand all mysteries and all knowledge, and if I have all faith so that I can move mountains but do not have love, I am nothing. [3] And if I give away all my possessions, and if I give over my body in order to boast but do not have love, I gain nothing.

[4] Love is patient, love is kind. Love does not envy, is not boastful, is not arrogant, [5] is not rude, is not self-seeking, is not irritable, and does not keep a record of wrongs. [6] Love finds no joy in unrighteousness but rejoices in the truth. [7] It bears all things, believes all things, hopes all things, endures all things.

[8] Love never ends. But as for prophecies, they will come to an end; as for tongues, they will cease; as for knowledge, it will come to an end. [9] For we know in part, and we prophesy in part, [10] but when the perfect comes, the partial will come to an end. [11] When I was a child, I spoke like a child, I thought like a child, I reasoned like a child. When I became a man, I put aside childish things. [12] For now we see only a reflection as in a mirror, but then face to face. Now I know in part, but then I will know fully, as I am fully known. [13] Now these three remain: faith, hope, and love—but the greatest of these is love.

GALATIANS 6:1-2, 10

[1] Brothers and sisters, if someone is overtaken in any wrongdoing, you who are spiritual, restore such a person with a gentle spirit, watching out for yourselves so that you also won't be tempted. [2] Carry one another's burdens; in this way you will fulfill the law of Christ.

…

[10] Therefore, as we have opportunity, let us work for the good of all, especially for those who belong to the household of faith.

COLOSSIANS 3:9-15

[9] Do not lie to one another, since you have put off the old self with its practices [10] and have put on the new self. You are being renewed in knowledge according to the image of your Creator. [11] In Christ there is not Greek and Jew, circumcision and uncircumcision, barbarian, Scythian, slave and free; but Christ is all and in all.

THE CHRISTIAN LIFE

[12] Therefore, as God's chosen ones, holy and dearly loved, put on compassion, kindness, humility, gentleness, and patience, [13] bearing with one another and forgiving one another if anyone has a grievance against another. Just as the Lord has forgiven you, so you are also to forgive. [14] Above all, put on love, which is the perfect bond of unity. [15] And let the peace of Christ, to which you were also called in one body, rule your hearts. And be thankful.

Key Verse

For this reason, although I have great boldness in Christ to command you to do what is right, I appeal to you, instead, on the basis of love.

PHILEMON 8–9a

HOW PHILEMON FITS IN THE STORY

Philemon is Paul's shortest letter, yet it is considered one of his most heartfelt. It also captures the true heart of the gospel. When we come to God in repentance and faith, He gives us a new status in the family of God. He welcomes us as if we were Jesus, who assumed full responsibility for the debt of our sin.

COPY PHILEMON 8–9a INTO THE SPACE PROVIDED ON PAGE 188.

1   What do Paul's words in today's reading teach you about forgiveness and reconciliation among believers?

2   How does today's reading shape your understanding of the story of redemption?

RESPONSE

*Therefore, since we also have such a large cloud of witnesses surrounding us,
let us lay aside every hindrance and the sin that so easily ensnares us. Let us run
with endurance the race that lies before us, keeping our eyes on Jesus, the pioneer
and perfecter of our faith. For the joy that lay before him, he endured the cross,
despising the shame, and sat down at the right hand of the throne of God.*

HEBREWS 12:1–2

General Epistles

Hebrews

WHAT IS HEBREWS?

Written by an unknown author, the book of Hebrews explores the majesty and supremacy of Jesus over all things. It connects Israel's rich history and the Pentateuch to the work of Jesus, our High Priest. Hebrews details how Jesus is the fulfillment of the law and all of God's promises in the Old Testament.

HEBREWS 10:19–25, 32–39
EXHORTATIONS TO GODLINESS

[19] Therefore, brothers and sisters, since we have boldness to enter the sanctuary through the blood of Jesus— [20] he has inaugurated for us a new and living way through the curtain (that is, through his flesh)— [21] and since we have a great high priest over the house of God, [22] let us draw near with a true heart in full assurance of faith, with our hearts sprinkled clean from an evil conscience and our bodies washed in pure water. [23] Let us hold on to the confession of our hope without wavering, since he who promised is faithful. [24] And let us consider one another in order to provoke love and good works, [25] not neglecting to gather together, as some are in the habit of doing, but encouraging each other, and all the more as you see the day approaching.

…

[32] Remember the earlier days when, after you had been enlightened, you endured a hard struggle with sufferings. [33] Sometimes you were publicly exposed to taunts and afflictions, and at other times you were companions of those who were treated that way. [34] For you sympathized with the prisoners and accepted with joy the confiscation of your possessions, because you know that you yourselves have a better and enduring possession. [35] So don't throw away your confidence, which has a great reward. [36] For you need endurance, so that after you have done God's will, you may receive what was promised.

[37] For yet in a very little while,
the Coming One will come and not delay.
[38] But my righteous one will live by faith;
and if he draws back,
I have no pleasure in him.

[39] But we are not those who draw back and are destroyed, but those who have faith and are saved.

HEBREWS 12:1–13

THE CALL TO ENDURANCE

KEY VERSE

¹ Therefore, since we also have such a large cloud of witnesses surrounding us, let us lay aside every hindrance and the sin that so easily ensnares us. Let us run with endurance the race that lies before us, ² keeping our eyes on Jesus, the pioneer and perfecter of our faith. For the joy that lay before him, he endured the cross, despising the shame, and sat down at the right hand of the throne of God.

FATHERLY DISCIPLINE

³ For consider him who endured such hostility from sinners against himself, so that you won't grow weary and give up. ⁴ In struggling against sin, you have not yet resisted to the point of shedding your blood. ⁵ And you have forgotten the exhortation that addresses you as sons:

> My son, do not take the Lord's discipline lightly
> or lose heart when you are reproved by him,
> ⁶ for the Lord disciplines the one he loves
> and punishes every son he receives.

⁷ Endure suffering as discipline: God is dealing with you as sons. For what son is there that a father does not discipline? ⁸ But if you are without discipline—which all receive—then you are illegitimate children and not sons. ⁹ Furthermore, we had human fathers discipline us, and we respected them. Shouldn't we submit even more to the Father of spirits and live? ¹⁰ For they disciplined us for a short time based on what seemed good to them, but he does it for our benefit, so that we can share his holiness. ¹¹ No discipline seems enjoyable at the time, but painful. Later on, however, it yields the peaceful fruit of righteousness to those who have been trained by it.

¹² Therefore, strengthen your tired hands and weakened knees, ¹³ and make straight paths for your feet, so that what is lame may not be dislocated but healed instead.

JOB 5:17–18

¹⁷ See how happy is the person whom God corrects;
so do not reject the discipline of the Almighty.
¹⁸ For he wounds but he also bandages;
he strikes, but his hands also heal.

PROVERBS 3:11–12

[11] Do not despise the LORD's instruction, my son,
and do not loathe his discipline;
[12] for the LORD disciplines the one he loves,
just as a father disciplines the son in whom he delights.

1 CORINTHIANS 9:24–27

[24] Don't you know that the runners in a stadium all race, but only one receives the prize? Run in such a way to win the prize. [25] Now everyone who competes exercises self-control in everything. They do it to receive a perishable crown, but we an imperishable crown. [26] So I do not run like one who runs aimlessly or box like one beating the air. [27] Instead, I discipline my body and bring it under strict control, so that after preaching to others, I myself will not be disqualified.

PHILIPPIANS 3:12–21
REACHING FORWARD TO GOD'S GOAL

[12] Not that I have already reached the goal or am already perfect, but I make every effort to take hold of it because I also have been taken hold of by Christ Jesus. [13] Brothers and sisters, I do not consider myself to have taken hold of it. But one thing I do: Forgetting what is behind and reaching forward to what is ahead, [14] I pursue as my goal the prize promised by God's heavenly call in Christ Jesus. [15] Therefore, let all of us who are mature think this way. And if you think differently about anything, God will reveal this also to you. [16] In any case, we should live up to whatever truth we have attained. [17] Join in imitating me, brothers and sisters, and pay careful attention to those who live according to the example you have in us. [18] For I have often told you, and now say again with tears, that many live as enemies of the cross of Christ. [19] Their end is destruction; their god is their stomach; their glory is in their shame; and they are focused on earthly things. [20] Our citizenship is in heaven, and we eagerly wait for a Savior from there, the Lord Jesus Christ. [21] He will transform the body of our humble condition into the likeness of his glorious body, by the power that enables him to subject everything to himself.

Key Verse

Therefore, since we also have such a large cloud of witnesses surrounding us, let us lay aside every hindrance and the sin that so easily ensnares us. Let us run with endurance the race that lies before us, keeping our eyes on Jesus, the pioneer and perfecter of our faith. For the joy that lay before him, he endured the cross, despising the shame, and sat down at the right hand of the throne of God.

HEBREWS 12:1–2

HOW HEBREWS FITS IN THE STORY

Hebrews ties Old Testament history and practices to the life and ministry of Jesus more than any other book in the New Testament. Just as Jesus taught that the Old Testament has been fulfilled in Him, Hebrews shows how the old covenant was fulfilled and the new covenant has been extended to us in Him. This glorious future, secured for us in Christ Jesus, gives us a reason to endure in the faith.

COPY HEBREWS 12:1–2 INTO THE SPACE PROVIDED ON PAGE 189.

1 What "race" do you think the author is referring to in Hebrews 12:1–2? How do you keep your eyes on Jesus as you "run"?

2 How does today's reading shape your understanding of the story of redemption?

RESPONSE

JESUS PAID IT ALL, ALL TO HIM I OWE;

SIN HAD LEFT A CRIMSON STAIN,

HE WASHED IT WHITE AS SNOW.

Hymn

Jesus Paid It All

WORDS
Elvina M. Hall, 1865

MUSIC
John T. Grape, 1868

1. I___ hear the Sa - vior say, "Thy stength in - deed is small,
2. Lord,___ now in - deed I find Thy pow'r and Thine a - lone,
3. For___ noth - ing good have I where - by Thy grace to claim;
4. And___ when, be - fore the throne, I stand in Him com - plete,

Child of weak - ness, watch and pray, Find in Me thine all in all."
Can___ change the le - per's spots and___ melt the heart of stone.
I'll___ wash my gar - ments white in the blood of Cal - v'ry's Lamb.
"Je - sus died my soul to save," my ___ lips shall still re - peat.

Refrain

Je - sus paid it all, All to Him I owe;

Sin had left a crim - son stain, He washed it white as snow.

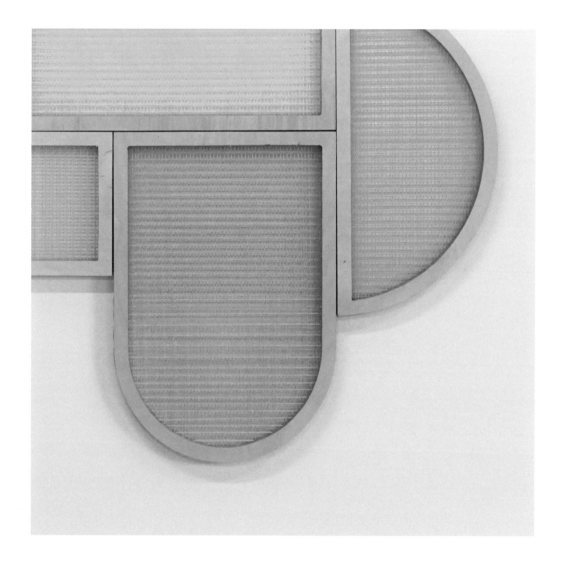

Consider it a great joy, my brothers and sisters, whenever you experience various trials, because you know that the testing of your faith produces endurance. And let endurance have its full effect, so that you may be mature and complete, lacking nothing.

JAMES 1:2–4

General Epistles

James

WHAT IS JAMES?

Written by James, the brother of Jesus, this book instructs and admonishes readers to seek godly wisdom. It also counsels them to avoid internal conflicts within the Church and to express their faith through good works. James encourages believers to persevere in this calling in spite of trials, as God is faithful to mature His people in the midst of suffering.

JAMES 1:1–18

¹ James, a servant of God and of the Lord Jesus Christ:

To the twelve tribes dispersed abroad.

Greetings.

TRIALS AND MATURITY

KEY VERSE

² Consider it a great joy, my brothers and sisters, whenever you experience various trials, ³ because you know that the testing of your faith produces endurance. ⁴ And let endurance have its full effect, so that you may be mature and complete, lacking nothing.

⁵ Now if any of you lacks wisdom, he should ask God—who gives to all generously and ungrudgingly—and it will be given to him. ⁶ But let him ask in faith without doubting. For

the doubter is like the surging sea, driven and tossed by the wind. [7] That person should not expect to receive anything from the Lord, [8] being double-minded and unstable in all his ways.

[9] Let the brother of humble circumstances boast in his exaltation, [10] but let the rich boast in his humiliation because he will pass away like a flower of the field. [11] For the sun rises and, together with the scorching wind, dries up the grass; its flower falls off, and its beautiful appearance perishes. In the same way, the rich person will wither away while pursuing his activities.

[12] Blessed is the one who endures trials, because when he has stood the test he will receive the crown of life that God has promised to those who love him.

[13] No one undergoing a trial should say, "I am being tempted by God," since God is not tempted by evil, and he himself doesn't tempt anyone. [14] But each person is tempted when he is drawn away and enticed by his own evil desire. [15] Then after desire has conceived, it gives birth to sin, and when sin is fully grown, it gives birth to death.

[16] Don't be deceived, my dear brothers and sisters. [17] Every good and perfect gift is from above, coming down from the Father of lights, who does not change like shifting shadows. [18] By his own choice, he gave us birth by the word of truth so that we would be a kind of firstfruits of his creatures.

GENESIS 50:15–21

JOSEPH'S KINDNESS

[15] When Joseph's brothers saw that their father was dead, they said to one another, "If Joseph is holding a grudge against us, he will certainly repay us for all the suffering we caused him."

[16] So they sent this message to Joseph, "Before he died your father gave a command: [17] 'Say this to Joseph: Please forgive your brothers' transgression and their sin—the suffering they caused you.' Therefore, please forgive the transgression of the servants of the God of your father." Joseph wept when their message came to him. [18] His brothers also came to him, bowed down before him, and said, "We are your slaves!"

[19] But Joseph said to them, "Don't be afraid. Am I in the place of God? [20] You planned evil against me; God planned it for good to bring about the present result—the survival of many people. [21] Therefore don't be afraid. I will take care of you and your children." And he comforted them and spoke kindly to them.

JOHN 16:33

"I have told you these things so that in me you may have peace. You will have suffering in this world. Be courageous! I have conquered the world."

ROMANS 8:18–23

FROM GROANS TO GLORY

[18] For I consider that the sufferings of this present time are not worth comparing with the glory that is going to be revealed to us. [19] For the creation eagerly waits with anticipation for God's sons to be revealed. [20] For the creation was subjected to futility—not willingly, but because of him who subjected it—in the hope [21] that the creation itself will also be set free from the bondage to decay into the glorious freedom of God's children. [22] For we know that the whole creation has been groaning together with labor pains until now. [23] Not only that, but we ourselves who have the Spirit as the firstfruits—we also groan within ourselves, eagerly waiting for adoption, the redemption of our bodies.

1 PETER 4:12–19

CHRISTIAN SUFFERING

[12] Dear friends, don't be surprised when the fiery ordeal comes among you to test you, as if something unusual were happening to you. [13] Instead, rejoice as you share in the sufferings of Christ, so that you may also rejoice with great joy when his glory is revealed. [14] If you are ridiculed for the name of Christ, you are blessed, because the Spirit of glory and of God rests on you. [15] Let none of you suffer as a murderer, a thief, an evildoer, or a meddler. [16] But if anyone suffers as a Christian, let him not be ashamed but let him glorify God in having that name. [17] For the time has come for judgment to begin with God's household, and if it begins with us, what will the outcome be for those who disobey the gospel of God?

> [18] And if a righteous person is saved with difficulty,
> what will become of the ungodly and the sinner?

[19] So then, let those who suffer according to God's will entrust themselves to a faithful Creator while doing what is good.

DAY 26: JAMES

Key Verse

Consider it a great joy, my brothers and sisters, whenever you experience various trials, because you know that the testing of your faith produces endurance. And let endurance have its full effect, so that you may be mature and complete, lacking nothing.

JAMES 1:2-4

HOW JAMES FITS IN THE STORY

James continually calls for obedience to the law of God, showing believers that their obedience to God's instruction is an indication of a living faith. Some choose to oversimplify the distinctions between the Old Testament and the New Testament by saying that the Old Testament is grounded in works and the New Testament is grounded in faith. James brings both testaments together to show that faith and works are integrally related in both the old and new covenants.

COPY JAMES 1:2-4 INTO THE SPACE PROVIDED ON PAGE 189.

1 Why does James say to be joyful during trials? Practically, how can you express joy in the middle of your current challenges?

2 How does today's reading shape your understanding of the story of redemption?

RESPONSE

Peach Crumble

Ingredients

PEACH FILLING

4 cups fresh peaches, chopped or diced

2 tablespoons cornstarch

3 tablespoons brown sugar

1 teaspoon vanilla extract

CRUMBLE TOPPING

¼ cup brown sugar

½ cup old fashioned oats

1 tablespoon all purpose flour

4 tablespoons cold butter

Instructions

Preheat oven to 350°F.

Combine peaches with cornstarch, brown sugar, and vanilla. Place peach filling into an 8x8 greased baking dish.

Make the crumble topping by using your hands or a wooden spatula to mix ingredients until crumbly. Spread crumble on top of filling in baking dish.

Bake for 30 minutes. Remove from oven. Dish into 4-ounce mason jars. Serve with ice cream on top and enjoy!

THIS IS THE NEW TESTAMENT

DAY 27

GRACE DAY

Take this day to catch up on your reading,
pray, and rest in the presence of the Lord.

He will again have compassion
on us; he will vanquish our
iniquities. You will cast all our
sins into the depths of the sea.

MICAH 7:19

DAY 28

WEEKLY TRUTH

Scripture is God-breathed and true. When we memorize it, we carry the good news of Jesus with us wherever we go.

So far in our survey, we've memorized Acts 13:27–29. This week, we'll add verses 30 and 31, where the risen Christ continues His ministry. Copy the verses into the space provided as you commit them to memory.

But God raised him from the dead, and he appeared for many days to those who came up with him from Galilee to Jerusalem, who are now his witnesses to the people.

ACTS 13:30–31

NOTES

DAY 29

General Epistles

1 Peter

WHAT IS 1 PETER?

The book of 1 Peter was written by Peter, one of Jesus's disciples, to encourage persecuted Gentile Christians living in Asia Minor (modern-day Turkey). He calls them to stand firm in their faith, abandoning their idolatrous behavior for righteous living in Christ. First Peter centers around the living hope and new life offered to us in the resurrected Jesus.

1 PETER 1:3-25
A LIVING HOPE

[KEY VERSE]

[3] Blessed be the God and Father of our Lord Jesus Christ. Because of his great mercy he has given us new birth into a living hope through the resurrection of Jesus Christ from the dead [4] and into an inheritance that is imperishable, undefiled, and unfading, kept in heaven for you.

[5] You are being guarded by God's power through faith for a salvation that is ready to be revealed in the last time. [6] You rejoice in this, even though now for a short time, if necessary, you suffer grief in various trials [7] so that the proven character of your faith—more valuable than gold which, though perishable, is refined by fire—may result in praise, glory, and honor at the revelation of Jesus Christ. [8] Though you have not seen him, you love him; though not seeing him now, you

believe in him, and you rejoice with inexpressible and glorious joy, [9] because you are receiving the goal of your faith, the salvation of your souls.

[10] Concerning this salvation, the prophets, who prophesied about the grace that would come to you, searched and carefully investigated. [11] They inquired into what time or what circumstances the Spirit of Christ within them was indicating when he testified in advance to the sufferings of Christ and the glories that would follow. [12] It was revealed to them that they were not serving themselves but you. These things have now been announced to you through those who preached the gospel to you by the Holy Spirit sent from heaven—angels long to catch a glimpse of these things.

A CALL TO HOLY LIVING

[13] Therefore, with your minds ready for action, be sober-minded and set your hope completely on the grace to be brought to you at the revelation of Jesus Christ. [14] As obedient children, do not be conformed to the desires of your former ignorance. [15] But as the one who called you is holy, you also are to be holy in all your conduct; [16] for it is written, Be holy, because I am holy. [17] If you appeal to the Father who judges impartially according to each one's work, you are to conduct yourselves in reverence during your time living as strangers. [18] For you know that you were redeemed from your empty way of life inherited from your ancestors, not with perishable things like silver or gold, [19] but with the precious blood of Christ, like that of an unblemished and spotless lamb. [20] He was foreknown before the foundation of the world but was revealed in these last times for you. [21] Through him you believe in God, who raised him from the dead and gave him glory, so that your faith and hope are in God.

[22] Since you have purified yourselves by your obedience to the truth, so that you show sincere brotherly love for each other, from a pure heart love one another constantly, [23] because you have been born again—not of perishable seed but of imperishable—through the living and enduring word of God. [24] For

> All flesh is like grass,
> and all its glory like a flower of the grass.
> The grass withers, and the flower falls,
> [25] but the word of the Lord endures forever.

And this word is the gospel that was proclaimed to you.

LEVITICUS 20:7–8

[7] "Consecrate yourselves and be holy, for I am the Lᴏʀᴅ your God. [8] Keep my statutes and do them; I am the Lᴏʀᴅ who sets you apart."

FAITH TRIUMPHS

[1] Therefore, since we have been justified by faith, we have peace with God through our Lord Jesus Christ. [2] We have also obtained access through him by faith into this grace in which we stand, and we boast in the hope of the glory of God. [3] And not only that, but we also boast in our afflictions, because we know that affliction produces endurance, [4] endurance produces proven character, and proven character produces hope. [5] This hope will not disappoint us, because God's love has been poured out in our hearts through the Holy Spirit who was given to us.

THE JUSTIFIED ARE RECONCILED

[6] For while we were still helpless, at the right time, Christ died for the ungodly. [7] For rarely will someone die for a just person—though for a good person perhaps someone might even dare to die. [8] But God proves his own love for us in that while we were still sinners, Christ died for us. [9] How much more then, since we have now been justified by his blood, will we be saved through him from wrath. [10] For if, while we were enemies, we were reconciled to God through the death of his Son, then how much more, having been reconciled, will we be saved by his life. [11] And not only that, but we also boast in God through our Lord Jesus Christ, through whom we have now received this reconciliation.

Key Verse

Blessed be the God and Father of our Lord Jesus Christ. Because of his great mercy he has given us new birth into a living hope through the resurrection of Jesus Christ from the dead and into an inheritance that is imperishable, undefiled, and unfading, kept in heaven for you.

1 PETER 1:3-4

HOW 1 PETER FITS IN THE STORY

First Peter proclaims that believers have a secure heavenly hope and eternal inheritance. Peter's message of encouragement in the face of suffering calls us to live lives of love and holiness, glorifying God by imitating Jesus no matter the circumstance.

COPY 1 PETER 1:3-4 INTO THE SPACE PROVIDED ON PAGE 190.

1 What is the "proven character" of our faith described in 1 Peter 1:6–7, and what does it accomplish in Christ?

2 How does today's reading shape your understanding of the story of redemption?

RESPONSE

*His divine power has given us everything required for life and godliness through
the knowledge of him who called us by his own glory and goodness.*

2 PETER 1:3

General Epistles

2 Peter

WHAT IS 2 PETER?

In 2 Peter, the apostle Peter cautions believers against false teachers and immoral behavior. He also emphasizes Christ's second coming and the importance of an active, growing faith as we await Christ's return.

2 PETER 1:3–21
GROWTH IN THE FAITH

KEY VERSE

³ His divine power has given us everything required for life and godliness through the knowledge of him who called us by his own glory and goodness.

⁴ By these he has given us very great and precious promises, so that through them you may share in the divine nature, escaping the corruption that is in the world because of evil desire. ⁵ For this very reason, make every effort to supplement your faith with goodness, goodness with knowledge, ⁶ knowledge with self-control, self-control with endurance, endurance with godliness, ⁷ godliness with brotherly affection, and brotherly affection with love. ⁸ For if you possess these qualities in increasing measure, they will keep you from being useless or unfruitful in the knowledge of our Lord Jesus Christ. ⁹ The person who lacks these things is blind and shortsighted and has forgotten the cleansing from his past sins. ¹⁰ Therefore, brothers and sisters, make

every effort to confirm your calling and election, because if you do these things you will never stumble. [11] For in this way, entry into the eternal kingdom of our Lord and Savior Jesus Christ will be richly provided for you.

[12] Therefore I will always remind you about these things, even though you know them and are established in the truth you now have. [13] I think it is right, as long as I am in this bodily tent, to wake you up with a reminder, [14] since I know that I will soon lay aside my tent, as our Lord Jesus Christ has indeed made clear to me. [15] And I will also make every effort so that you are able to recall these things at any time after my departure.

THE TRUSTWORTHY PROPHETIC WORD

[16] For we did not follow cleverly contrived myths when we made known to you the power and coming of our Lord Jesus Christ; instead, we were eyewitnesses of his majesty. [17] For he received honor and glory from God the Father when the voice came to him from the Majestic Glory, saying "This is my beloved Son, with whom I am well-pleased!" [18] We ourselves heard this voice when it came from heaven while we were with him on the holy mountain. [19] We also have the prophetic word strongly confirmed, and you will do well to pay attention to it, as to a lamp shining in a dark place, until the day dawns and the morning star rises in your hearts. [20] Above all, you know this: No prophecy of Scripture comes from the prophet's own interpretation, [21] because no prophecy ever came by the will of man; instead, men spoke from God as they were carried along by the Holy Spirit.

PROVERBS 1:7

The fear of the LORD
is the beginning of knowledge;
fools despise wisdom and discipline.

HEBREWS 6:1–7
WARNING AGAINST FALLING AWAY

[1] Therefore, let us leave the elementary teaching about Christ and go on to maturity, not laying again a foundation of repentance from dead works, faith in God, [2] teaching about ritual washings, laying on of hands, the resurrection of the dead, and eternal judgment. [3] And we will do this if God permits.

[4] For it is impossible to renew to repentance those who were once enlightened, who tasted the heavenly gift, who shared in the Holy Spirit, [5] who tasted God's good word and the powers of the coming age, [6] and who have fallen away. This is because, to their own harm, they are recrucifying the Son of God and holding him up to contempt. [7] For the ground that drinks the rain that often falls on it and that produces vegetation useful to those for whom it is cultivated receives a blessing from God.

[14] What good is it, my brothers and sisters, if someone claims to have faith but does not have works? Can such faith save him?

[15] If a brother or sister is without clothes and lacks daily food [16] and one of you says to them, "Go in peace, stay warm, and be well fed," but you don't give them what the body needs, what good is it? [17] In the same way faith, if it does not have works, is dead by itself.

[18] But someone will say, "You have faith, and I have works." Show me your faith without works, and I will show you faith by my works. [19] You believe that God is one. Good! Even the demons believe—and they shudder.

[20] Senseless person! Are you willing to learn that faith without works is useless? [21] Wasn't Abraham our father justified by works in offering Isaac his son on the altar? [22] You see that faith was active together with his works, and by works, faith was made complete, [23] and the Scripture was fulfilled that says, Abraham believed God, and it was credited to him as righteousness, and he was called God's friend. [24] You see that a person is justified by works and not by faith alone. [25] In the same way, wasn't Rahab the prostitute also justified by works in receiving the messengers and sending them out by a different route? [26] For just as the body without the spirit is dead, so also faith without works is dead.

Key Verse

His divine power has given us everything required for life and godliness through the knowledge of him who called us by his own glory and goodness.

2 PETER 1:3

HOW 2 PETER FITS IN THE STORY

Second Peter is strongly tied to the Old Testament. In it, Peter highlights the significance of God's Word through statements on the origin of Scripture, as well as the inspired nature of Paul's letters. Peter challenges his audience to live with authenticity, clinging to Scripture as the guide for faithful living.

COPY 2 PETER 1:3 INTO THE SPACE PROVIDED ON PAGE 190.

1 What are some characteristics of a believer who is growing in the Christian faith? According to 2 Peter 1:3–21, how does God's power help us grow in spiritual maturity?

2 How does today's reading shape your understanding of the story of redemption?

RESPONSE

A Matter of Time

Reading Through the New Testament

Over the past several weeks, we have been reading thematic selections from each New Testament book. While there is benefit to studying a particular passage or even a single verse, reading an entire book of the Bible in one sitting can help you see the author's progression of thought and make connections that might otherwise be missed.

Here is a look at how long it might take an average reader to read each book in the New Testament.

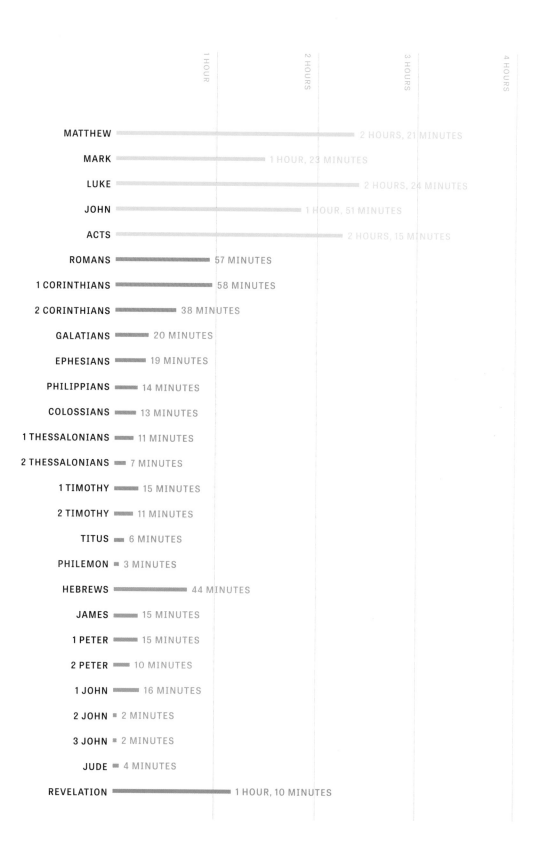

	1 HOUR	2 HOURS	3 HOURS	4 HOURS
MATTHEW		2 HOURS, 21 MINUTES		
MARK	1 HOUR, 23 MINUTES			
LUKE		2 HOURS, 24 MINUTES		
JOHN	1 HOUR, 51 MINUTES			
ACTS		2 HOURS, 15 MINUTES		
ROMANS	57 MINUTES			
1 CORINTHIANS	58 MINUTES			
2 CORINTHIANS	38 MINUTES			
GALATIANS	20 MINUTES			
EPHESIANS	19 MINUTES			
PHILIPPIANS	14 MINUTES			
COLOSSIANS	13 MINUTES			
1 THESSALONIANS	11 MINUTES			
2 THESSALONIANS	7 MINUTES			
1 TIMOTHY	15 MINUTES			
2 TIMOTHY	11 MINUTES			
TITUS	6 MINUTES			
PHILEMON	3 MINUTES			
HEBREWS	44 MINUTES			
JAMES	15 MINUTES			
1 PETER	15 MINUTES			
2 PETER	10 MINUTES			
1 JOHN	16 MINUTES			
2 JOHN	2 MINUTES			
3 JOHN	2 MINUTES			
JUDE	4 MINUTES			
REVELATION	1 HOUR, 10 MINUTES			

1, 2 & 3 John

WHAT ARE 1, 2 & 3 JOHN?

Written by the apostle John, the books of 1, 2 & 3 John describe how believers are to walk in true fellowship with God, actively loving their brothers and sisters in the faith. He writes in these three letters that it is the Holy Spirit who enables us to live this obedient life.

1 JOHN 1:5–10
FELLOWSHIP WITH GOD

⁵ This is the message we have heard from him and declare to you: God is light, and there is absolutely no darkness in him. ⁶ If we say, "We have fellowship with him," and yet we walk in darkness, we are lying and are not practicing the truth. ⁷ If we walk in the light as he himself is in the light, we have fellowship with one another, and the blood of Jesus his Son cleanses us from all sin. ⁸ If we say, "We have no sin," we are deceiving ourselves, and the truth is not in us.

KEY VERSE

⁹ If we confess our sins, he is faithful and righteous to forgive us our sins and to cleanse us from all unrighteousness.

¹⁰ If we say, "We have not sinned," we make him a liar, and his word is not in us.

2 JOHN 4–11
TRUTH AND DECEPTION

⁴ I was very glad to find some of your children walking in truth, in keeping with a command we have received from

the Father. [5] So now I ask you, dear lady—not as if I were writing you a new command, but one we have had from the beginning—that we love one another.

KEY VERSE

[6] **This is love: that we walk according to his commands. This is the command as you have heard it from the beginning: that you walk in love.**

[7] Many deceivers have gone out into the world; they do not confess the coming of Jesus Christ in the flesh. This is the deceiver and the antichrist. [8] Watch yourselves so that you don't lose what we have worked for, but that you may receive a full reward. [9] Anyone who does not remain in Christ's teaching but goes beyond it does not have God. The one who remains in that teaching, this one has both the Father and the Son. [10] If anyone comes to you and does not bring this teaching, do not receive him into your home, and do not greet him; [11] for the one who greets him shares in his evil works.

3 JOHN 1–8
GREETING

[1] The elder:

To my dear friend Gaius, whom I love in the truth.

[2] Dear friend, I pray that you are prospering in every way and are in good health, just as your whole life is going well. [3] For I was very glad when fellow believers came and testified to your fidelity to the truth—how you are walking in truth.

KEY VERSE

[1] **I have no greater joy than this: to hear that my children are walking in truth.**

GAIUS COMMENDED

[5] Dear friend, you are acting faithfully in whatever you do for the brothers and sisters, especially when they are strangers. [6] They have testified to your love before the church. You will do well to send them on their journey in a manner worthy of God, [7] since they set out for the sake of the Name, accepting nothing from pagans. [8] Therefore, we ought to support such people so that we can be coworkers with the truth.

DEUTERONOMY 15:10–11

[10] "Give to him, and don't have a stingy heart when you give, and because of this the Lord your God will bless you in all your work and in everything you do. [11] For there will never cease to be poor people in the land; that is why I am commanding you, 'Open your hand willingly to your poor and needy brother in your land.'"

PSALM 15
A DESCRIPTION OF THE GODLY

A psalm of David.

[1] Lord, who can dwell in your tent?
Who can live on your holy mountain?

[2] The one who lives blamelessly, practices righteousness,
and acknowledges the truth in his heart—
[3] who does not slander with his tongue,
who does not harm his friend
or discredit his neighbor,
[4] who despises the one rejected by the Lord
but honors those who fear the Lord,
who keeps his word whatever the cost,
[5] who does not lend his silver at interest
or take a bribe against the innocent—
the one who does these things will never be shaken.

MATTHEW 22:34–40
THE PRIMARY COMMANDS

[34] When the Pharisees heard that he had silenced the Sadducees, they came together. [35] And one of them, an expert in the law, asked a question to test him: [36] "Teacher, which command in the law is the greatest?"

[37] He said to him, "Love the Lord your God with all your heart, with all your soul, and with all your mind. [38] This is the greatest and most important command. [39] The second is like it: Love your neighbor as yourself. [40] All the Law and the Prophets depend on these two commands."

Key Verses

If we confess our sins, he is faithful and righteous to forgive us our sins and to cleanse us from all unrighteousness.

1 JOHN 1:9

This is love: that we walk according to his commands. This is the command as you have heard it from the beginning: that you walk in love.

2 JOHN 6

I have no greater joy than this: to hear that my children are walking in truth.

3 JOHN 4

HOW 1, 2 & 3 JOHN FIT IN THE STORY

First John maps out the three main components of saving knowledge of God: faith in Jesus Christ, obedient response to God's commands, and true love for God and others. This letter shows how Jesus expects His followers to honor Him daily wherever they are.

Second John encourages believers to stay the course, responding to one another with love and the truth of the gospel. This letter challenges readers to remain steadfast in their faith and hope in Jesus Christ, eventually receiving a "full reward" from Him (2Jn 8).

Third John underscores central Christian convictions and testifies to the God-centeredness of the Christian faith. Jesus and the Holy Spirit are not mentioned specifically, but in the writer's view, both are included when referencing God in this letter (3Jn 1, 3–4, 8, 12).

COPY 1 JOHN 1:9, 2 JOHN 6, AND 3 JOHN 4 INTO THE SPACES PROVIDED ON PAGES 190 AND 191.

1 How do 1, 2 & 3 John speak to the relationship between genuine faith and loving others? In what area of your life do you struggle to show love to others?

2 How does today's reading shape your understanding of the story of redemption?

RESPONSE

Jude

WHAT IS JUDE?

Possibly written by the brother of Jesus and James, the book of Jude urges readers to steward their influence within the church by contending for the faith, remaining vigilant against heresy. They will maintain their unity by remembering their shared salvation in Christ.

JUDE

GREETING

¹ Jude, a servant of Jesus Christ and a brother of James:

To those who are the called, loved by God the Father and kept for Jesus Christ.

² May mercy, peace, and love be multiplied to you.

JUDE'S PURPOSE IN WRITING

³ Dear friends, although I was eager to write you about the salvation we share, I found it necessary to write, appealing to you to contend for the faith that was delivered to the saints once for all. ⁴ For some people, who were designated for this judgment long ago, have come in by stealth; they are ungodly, turning the grace of our God into sensuality and denying Jesus Christ, our only Master and Lord.

APOSTATES: PAST AND PRESENT

⁵ Now I want to remind you, although you came to know all these things once and for all, that Jesus saved a people out of Egypt and later destroyed those who did not believe; ⁶ and the angels who did not keep their own position but abandoned their proper dwelling, he has kept in eternal chains in deep darkness for the judgment on the great day. ⁷ Likewise, Sodom and Gomorrah and the surrounding towns committed sexual immorality and perversions, and serve as an example by undergoing the punishment of eternal fire.

⁸ In the same way these people—relying on their dreams—defile their flesh, reject authority, and slander glorious ones. ⁹ Yet when Michael the archangel was disputing with the devil in an argument about Moses's body, he did not dare utter a slanderous condemnation against him but said, "The Lord rebuke you!" ¹⁰ But these people blaspheme anything they do not understand. And what they do understand by instinct—like irrational animals—by these things they are destroyed. ¹¹ Woe to them! For they have gone the way of Cain, have plunged into Balaam's error for profit, and have perished in Korah's rebellion.

THE APOSTATES' DOOM

[12] These people are dangerous reefs at your love feasts as they eat with you without reverence. They are shepherds who only look after themselves. They are waterless clouds carried along by winds; trees in late autumn—fruitless, twice dead and uprooted. [13] They are wild waves of the sea, foaming up their shameful deeds; wandering stars for whom the blackness of darkness is reserved forever.

[14] It was about these that Enoch, in the seventh generation from Adam, prophesied: "Look! The Lord comes with tens of thousands of his holy ones [15] to execute judgment on all and to convict all the ungodly concerning all the ungodly acts that they have done in an ungodly way, and concerning all the harsh things ungodly sinners have said against him." [16] These people are discontented grumblers, living according to their desires; their mouths utter arrogant words, flattering people for their own advantage.

[17] But you, dear friends, remember what was predicted by the apostles of our Lord Jesus Christ. [18] They told you, "In the end time there will be scoffers living according to their own ungodly desires." [19] These people create divisions and are worldly, not having the Spirit.

EXHORTATION AND BENEDICTION

[20] But you, dear friends, as you build yourselves up in your most holy faith, praying in the Holy Spirit, [21] keep yourselves in the love of God, waiting expectantly for the mercy of our Lord Jesus Christ for eternal life. [22] Have mercy on those who waver; [23] save others by snatching them from the fire; have mercy on others but with fear, hating even the garment defiled by the flesh.

◆ KEY VERSE

[24] Now to him who is able to protect you from stumbling and to make you stand in the presence of his glory, without blemish and with great joy, [25] to the only God our Savior, through Jesus Christ our Lord, be glory, majesty, power, and authority before all time, now and forever. Amen.

ISAIAH 5:18–20

[18] "Woe to those who drag iniquity
with cords of deceit
and pull sin along with cart ropes,
[19] to those who say,
'Let him hurry up and do his work quickly
so that we can see it!
Let the plan of the Holy One of Israel take place
so that we can know it!'
[20] Woe to those who call evil good
and good evil,
who substitute darkness for light
and light for darkness,
who substitute bitter for sweet
and sweet for bitter."

1 TIMOTHY 6:12–14

[12] Fight the good fight of the faith. Take hold of eternal life to which you were called and about which you have made a good confession in the presence of many witnesses. [13] In the presence of God, who gives life to all, and of Christ Jesus, who gave a good confession before Pontius Pilate, I charge you [14] to keep this command without fault or failure until the appearing of our Lord Jesus Christ.

Key Verse

Now to him who is able to protect you from stumbling and to make you stand in the presence of his glory, without blemish and with great joy, to the only God our Savior, through Jesus Christ our Lord, be glory, majesty, power, and authority before all time, now and forever. Amen.

JUDE 24–25

HOW JUDE FITS IN THE STORY

The letter of Jude has often been overlooked by New Testament scholars because of its short length. However, its message is relevant to believers of every era. Jude sought to protect Christian truth and strongly opposed heretics who threatened the faith, and he called his readers to be just as passionate in their defense of the gospel.

COPY JUDE 24–25 INTO THE SPACE PROVIDED ON PAGE 191.

1 Based on today's reading in Jude, what are specific things we can do to remain faithful to Jesus and the gospel in the midst of persecution?

2 How does today's reading shape your understanding of the story of redemption?

RESPONSE

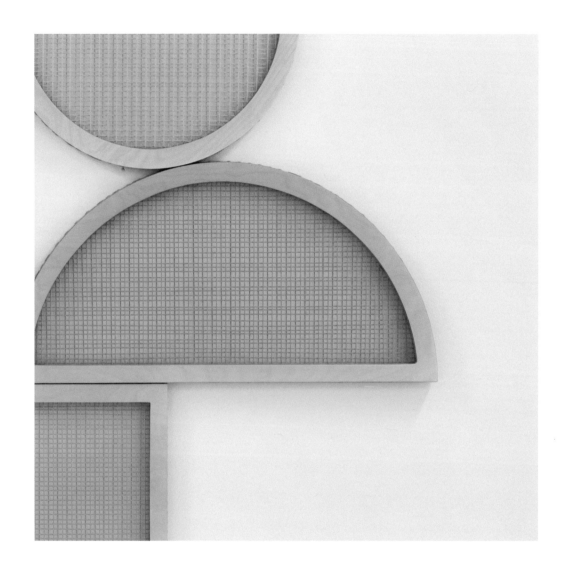

Then he said to me, "It is done! I am the Alpha and the Omega, the beginning and the end. I will freely give to the thirsty from the spring of the water of life."

REVELATION 21:6

Apocalyptic

Revelation

WHAT IS REVELATION?

The apostle John wrote the book of Revelation in exile on Patmos after receiving a vision from the Holy Spirit. The book of Revelation gives readers a picture of Jesus as the King who will one day return to usher in the fullness of His kingdom. Revelation offers important details about the ongoing work of the Holy Spirit, eternity in the presence of God, future judgment against sin, and the reality of the spiritual realm.

REVELATION 21
THE NEW CREATION

¹ Then I saw a new heaven and a new earth; for the first heaven and the first earth had passed away, and the sea was no more. ² I also saw the holy city, the new Jerusalem, coming down out of heaven from God, prepared like a bride adorned for her husband.

³ Then I heard a loud voice from the throne: Look, God's dwelling is with humanity, and he will live with them. They will be his peoples, and God himself will be with them and will be their God. ⁴ He will wipe away every tear from their eyes. Death will be no more; grief, crying, and pain will be no more, because the previous things have passed away.

⁵ Then the one seated on the throne said, "Look, I am making everything new." He also said, "Write, because these words are faithful and true."

⁶ Then he said to me, "It is done! I am the Alpha and the Omega, the beginning and the end. I will freely give to the thirsty from the spring of the water of life.

⁷ The one who conquers will inherit these things, and I will be his God, and he will be my son. ⁸ But the cowards, faithless, detestable, murderers, sexually immoral, sorcerers, idolaters, and all liars—their share will be in the lake that burns with fire and sulfur, which is the second death."

THE NEW JERUSALEM

⁹ Then one of the seven angels, who had held the seven bowls filled with the seven last plagues, came and spoke with me: "Come, I will show you the bride, the wife of the Lamb." ¹⁰ He then carried me away in the Spirit to a great, high mountain and showed me the holy city, Jerusalem, coming down out of heaven from God, ¹¹ arrayed with God's glory. Her radiance was like a precious jewel, like a jasper stone, clear as crystal. ¹² The city had a massive high wall, with twelve gates. Twelve angels were at the gates; the names of the twelve tribes of Israel's sons were inscribed on the gates. ¹³ There were three gates on the east, three gates on the north, three gates on the south, and three gates on the west. ¹⁴ The city wall had twelve foundations, and the twelve names of the twelve apostles of the Lamb were on the foundations.

¹⁵ The one who spoke with me had a golden measuring rod to measure the city, its gates, and its wall. ¹⁶ The city is laid out in a square; its length and width are the same. He measured the city with the rod at 12,000 *stadia*. Its length, width, and height are equal. ¹⁷ Then he measured its wall, 144 cubits according to human measurement, which the angel used. ¹⁸ The building material of its wall was jasper, and the city was pure gold clear as glass. ¹⁹ The foundations of the city wall were adorned with every kind of jewel: the first foundation is jasper, the second sapphire, the third chalcedony, the fourth emerald, ²⁰ the fifth sardonyx, the sixth carnelian, the seventh chrysolite, the eighth beryl, the ninth topaz, the tenth chrysoprase, the eleventh jacinth, the twelfth amethyst. ²¹ The twelve gates are twelve pearls; each individual gate was made of a single pearl. The main street of the city was pure gold, transparent as glass.

²² I did not see a temple in it, because the Lord God the Almighty and the Lamb are its temple. ²³ The city does not need the sun or the moon to shine on it, because the glory of God illuminates it, and its lamp is the Lamb. ²⁴ The nations will walk by its light, and the kings of the earth will bring their glory into it. ²⁵ Its gates will never close by day because it will never be night there. ²⁶ They will bring the glory and honor of the nations into it. ²⁷ Nothing unclean will ever enter it, nor anyone who does what is detestable or false, but only those written in the Lamb's book of life.

ISAIAH 65:17–25

A NEW CREATION

¹⁷ "For I will create new heavens and a new earth;
the past events will not be remembered or come to mind.
¹⁸ Then be glad and rejoice forever
in what I am creating;
for I will create Jerusalem to be a joy
and its people to be a delight.
¹⁹ I will rejoice in Jerusalem
and be glad in my people.
The sound of weeping and crying
will no longer be heard in her.
²⁰ In her, a nursing infant will no longer live
only a few days,
or an old man not live out his days.
Indeed, the one who dies at a hundred years old
will be mourned as a young man,
and the one who misses a hundred years
will be considered cursed.
²¹ People will build houses and live in them;
they will plant vineyards and eat their fruit.
²² They will not build and others live in them;
they will not plant and others eat.
For my people's lives will be
like the lifetime of a tree.
My chosen ones will fully enjoy
the work of their hands.
²³ They will not labor without success
or bear children destined for disaster,
for they will be a people blessed by the LORD
along with their descendants.

²⁴ Even before they call, I will answer;
while they are still speaking, I will hear.
²⁵ The wolf and the lamb will feed together,
and the lion will eat straw like cattle,
but the serpent's food will be dust!
They will not do what is evil or destroy
on my entire holy mountain,"
says the Lord.

EZEKIEL 37:26–27

²⁶ "I will make a covenant of peace with them; it will be a permanent covenant with them. I will establish and multiply them and will set my sanctuary among them forever. ²⁷ My dwelling place will be with them; I will be their God, and they will be my people."

Key Verse

Then he said to me, "It is done! I am the Alpha and the Omega, the beginning and the end. I will freely give to the thirsty from the spring of the water of life."

REVELATION 21:6

HOW REVELATION FITS IN THE STORY

The book of Revelation provides a theological overview of many topics central to Christian belief, including events surrounding the end times and the glorified Son of Man. It also stresses the practical choices that all people must make in light of eternity. Revelation provides a holistic view of Jesus as the victorious King of kings, one who is coming back for His bride. It also emphasizes the hope all believers share in His future return.

COPY REVELATION 21:6 INTO THE SPACE PROVIDED ON PAGE 192.

1 What do you find most hopeful about the description of the new Jerusalem in Revelation 21?

2 How does today's reading shape your understanding of the story of redemption?

RESPONSE

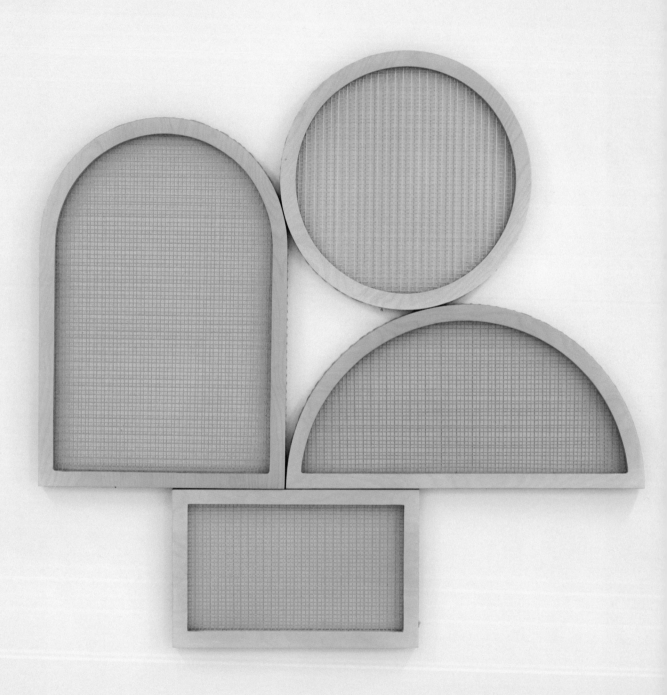

DAY 34

GRACE DAY

Take this day to catch up on your reading,
pray, and rest in the presence of the Lord.

"My dwelling place will be
with them; I will be their God,
and they will be my people."

EZEKIEL 37:27

DAY 35

WEEKLY TRUTH

Scripture is God-breathed and true. When we memorize it, we carry the good news of Jesus with us wherever we go.

Test your memory of Acts 13:27–31 by filling in the blanks on the right. Then recite the passage in full, reflecting on all you have learned in your survey of the New Testament.

²⁷ Since the _____ of _____ and their _____ did not _____ him or the sayings of the _____ that are read every _____, they have _____ their words by _____ him. ²⁸ Though they found no _____ for the _____ sentence, they asked _____ to have him _____. ²⁹ When they had carried out all that had been _____ about him, they took him down from the ____ and put him in a _____. ³⁰ But God _____ him from the _____, ³¹ and he _____ for many days to those who came up with him from _____ to Jerusalem, who are now his _____ to the people.

ACTS 13:27–31

New Testament

Key Verses

During this study, you've written a key verse for each book of the New Testament in the space provided. Together, these verses represent the New Testament portion of the complete arc of Scripture.

If you haven't already, pick up a **This Is the Old Testament** Study Book to continue this thematic journey through the Bible!

MATTHEW 4:17

MARK 10:45

LUKE 19:10

JOHN 1:1

ACTS 1:8

ROMANS 3:23-24

1 CORINTHIANS 1:9

2 CORINTHIANS 12:9

GALATIANS 2:21

EPHESIANS 2:8-9

PHILIPPIANS 1:21

COLOSSIANS 1:17

1 THESSALONIANS 5:16-18

2 THESSALONIANS 3:5

1 TIMOTHY 1:15

2 TIMOTHY 3:16–17

TITUS 3:5

PHILEMON 8–9a

HEBREWS 12:1-2

JAMES 1:2-4

1 PETER 1:3-4

2 PETER 1:3

1 JOHN 1:9

2 JOHN 6

---

3 JOHN 4

JUDE 24–25

THIS IS THE NEW TESTAMENT

BENEDICTION

Take time to read each key verse out loud. Today, and in the future, let this collection of verses serve as a reminder of the New Testament's contribution to the grand story of redemption.

CSB BOOK ABBREVIATIONS

OLD TESTAMENT

GN Genesis	**JB** Job	**HAB** Habakkuk	**PHP** Philippians
EX Exodus	**PS** Psalms	**ZPH** Zephaniah	**COL** Colossians
LV Leviticus	**PR** Proverbs	**HG** Haggai	**1TH** 1 Thessalonians
NM Numbers	**EC** Ecclesiastes	**ZCH** Zechariah	**2TH** 2 Thessalonians
DT Deuteronomy	**SG** Song of Solomon	**MAL** Malachi	**1TM** 1 Timothy
JOS Joshua	**IS** Isaiah		**2TM** 2 Timothy
JDG Judges	**JR** Jeremiah	NEW TESTAMENT	**TI** Titus
RU Ruth	**LM** Lamentations	**MT** Matthew	**PHM** Philemon
1SM 1 Samuel	**EZK** Ezekiel	**MK** Mark	**HEB** Hebrews
2SM 2 Samuel	**DN** Daniel	**LK** Luke	**JMS** James
1KG 1 Kings	**HS** Hosea	**JN** John	**1PT** 1 Peter
2KG 2 Kings	**JL** Joel	**AC** Acts	**2PT** 2 Peter
1CH 1 Chronicles	**AM** Amos	**RM** Romans	**1JN** 1 John
2CH 2 Chronicles	**OB** Obadiah	**1CO** 1 Corinthians	**2JN** 2 John
EZR Ezra	**JNH** Jonah	**2CO** 2 Corinthians	**3JN** 3 John
NEH Nehemiah	**MC** Micah	**GL** Galatians	**JD** Jude
EST Esther	**NAH** Nahum	**EPH** Ephesians	**RV** Revelation

BIBLIOGRAPHY

Bashaw, J. G. "Matthew the Apostle." In *The Lexham Bible Dictionary*. Logos Research Edition. Bellingham: Lexham Press, 2016.

Chase, Franklin J. "Judas, Brother of Jesus." In *The Lexham Bible Dictionary*. Logos Research Edition. Bellingham: Lexham Press, 2016.

Dicken, Frank E. "Luke." In *The Lexham Bible Dictionary*. Logos Research Edition. Bellingham: Lexham Press, 2016.

Gish, Jason. "Peter the Apostle." In *The Lexham Bible Dictionary*. Logos Research Edition. Bellingham: Lexham Press, 2016.

"Infographic: You Have More Time for Bible Reading Than You Think," Crossway, last modified November 19, 2018, https://www.crossway.org/articles/infographic-you-can-read-more-of-the-bible-than-you-think.

Le Donne, Anthony. "Paul the Apostle." In *The Lexham Bible Dictionary*. Logos Research Edition. Bellingham: Lexham Press, 2016.

Nässelqvist, Dan. "John the Apostle." In *The Lexham Bible Dictionary*. Logos Research Edition. Bellingham: Lexham Press, 2016.

Roudkovski, Viktor. "James, Brother of Jesus." In *The Lexham Bible Dictionary*. Logos Research Edition. Bellingham: Lexham Press, 2016.

Seal, David. "John Mark." In *The Lexham Bible Dictionary*. Logos Research Edition. Bellingham: Lexham Press, 2016.

LOOKING FOR
COMMUNITY DISCUSSION?

Download the **She Reads Truth app** to find a community of Shes reading right along with you. You can also share daily Scripture images and download free lock screens for Weekly Truth memorization—all on the She Reads Truth app.

DOWNLOAD THE
SHE READS TRUTH
APP TODAY!

FOR THE RECORD

WHERE DID I STUDY?

O HOME
O OFFICE
O COFFEE SHOP
O CHURCH
O A FRIEND'S HOUSE
O OTHER:

WHAT WAS I LISTENING TO?

ARTIST:

SONG:

PLAYLIST:

WHEN DID I STUDY?

O MORNING
O AFTERNOON
O NIGHT

HOW DID I FIND DELIGHT IN GOD'S WORD?

WHAT WAS HAPPENING IN MY LIFE?

WHAT WAS HAPPENING IN THE WORLD?

| MONTH | DAY | YEAR |

END DATE